THE CHURCH
A DEMON LOVER

A Sartrean Analysis
of an Institution

THE

CHURCH

A DEMON

LOVER

A Sartrean Analysis
of an Institution

by Roberta Imboden

University of Calgary Press

© 1995 Roberta A. Imboden

Canadian Cataloguing in Publication Data

Imboden, Roberta
    The church, a demon lover

    Includes bibliographical references and index.
    ISBN 1-895176-55-7

    1. Catholic Church—Government. 2. Catholic Church and
philosophy. 3. Sartre, Jean-Paul, 1905–1980—Political and social
views. I. Title.
BX1802.I42 1995   262'.02   C95-910321-X

COMMITTED TO THE DEVELOPMENT OF CULTURE AND THE ARTS

Printed and bound in Canada by Hignell Printing Limited.

♾ This book is printed on acid-free paper.

For my mother and Dave

A savage place!
As holy and enchanted
As e'er beneath a waning moon was haunted
By woman wailing for her demon lover!

Samuel Taylor Coleridge, "Kubla Khan" (1798)

Contents

Abbreviations

BN *Being and Nothingness*, by Jean-Paul Sartre, trans. Hazel E. Barnes (New York: Simon and Schuster, 1978).

CA *The Church in Anguish: Has the Vatican Betrayed Vatican II?*, ed. Hans Küng and Leonard J. Swidler (San Francisco: Harper & Row, 1986).

CDR, I *Critique of Dialectical Reason*, Vol. I, by Jean-Paul Sartre, trans. Alan Sheridan-Smith (London: New Left Books, 1976).

CDR, II *Critique of Dialectical Reason*, Vol. II, by Jean-Paul Sartre, trans. Quintin Hoare (London: Verso, 1991).

IMA *The Inquisition of the Middle Ages*, by Henry Charles Lea (London: Eyre and Spottiswoode, 1963).

MM *Malleus Maleficarium (The Hammer of the Witches)*, by Heinrich Institoris and Joseph Sprenger, trans. Montegue Summers (New York: B. Blom, 1970).

SC *Sartre's Second Critique*, by Ronald Aronson (Chicago: University of Chicago Press, 1987).

SM Search for a Method, by Jean-Paul Sartre, trans. Hazel E. Barnes (New York: Vintage Press, 1968).

TS *Trinity and Society*, by Leonardo Boff, trans. Paul Bruns (Maryknoll, NY: Orbis Books, 1988).

VC II *Vatican Council II: The Conciliar and Post Conciliar Documents*, ed. Austin Flannery, O.P. (1988 revised ed.; Northport, NY: Costello, 1975).

Acknowledgements

I would like to thank the following people for their support, discussion and critical reading: Charles Davis (Religious Studies, Concordia University), Andrian van den Hoven (Department of French, University of Windsor), Joanne McWilliam (Trinity Divinity School, University of Toronto), and Marie Dowler (Department of English, Ryerson Polytechnic University). I would like to thank Constance Luke for her support and suggestions and my husband David Grimshaw for his advice and forbearance and for his ability in aiding me with my struggles with the word processor.

This book has been published with the help of a grant from the Canadian Federation for the Humanities, using funds provided by the Social Sciences and Humanities Research Council of Canada.

Preface

The critique presented in this book, although accomplished through the conceptual apparatus of Jean-Paul Sartre, is not alien to some of the attitudes that permeate the postmodernist *Zeitgeist* of today's world. The foundation of this Sartrean analysis of the Roman Catholic Church is, above all, a critique of the structure of domination that belongs to every institution, but particularly to the Roman Church, since its extraordinary longevity causes its institutional characteristics to be more pronounced than those of any other institution in the world. It is the situation of domination that determines the basic praxis of the Church throughout history and, consequently, makes this praxis one of sado-masochism, rather than one of the love that is the message of Jesus Christ in the New Testament.

Another link between the basic thesis of this book and postmodernism is the concern with de-naturalizing some of the accepted features of our culture, such as capitalism and patriarchy. The attempt here is to denaturalize the structure of the Roman Church as it has existed for centuries, to make clear that there is nothing about the structure that is "natural" or God-given and cannot be changed. The point here is that the Roman Church does not reflect what Christianity truly is or should be; rather, it has created its own meaning for Christianity. Although we can attribute the existence of a Church to the dynamic energy of the Holy Spirit, we cannot attribute its structure to anything other than to the praxis of human beings. We, not God, have created this structure; therefore, this structure is open to critique. Thus, we must see this Church as the effect of the power of human beings, not as the effect of the love of God and, subsequently, as the source of the love of God.

In an associated theme with that of domination, this book also shares with postmodernism what some of their theorists see as the continuing of the unfinished project of the 1960s and its distrust of the ideologies of power. Here, there is certainly a direct link with the late Sartre, who took his philosophy into the streets and radicalized a whole generation of young French people. It was the model of this Sartre, more than anyone else, who inspired the French students to challenge all the institutions of France, a challenge that was the most effective and serious since that of the Commune of 1871.

Some critics of the postmodernist movement see it simply as a movement of decadence toward an unpalatable nihilism, but there are others who see it as an unsettling of old attitudes, dogmas, cultural givens and institutions which need to be altered, or even swept away. The hope is that this book will contribute to an unsettling that will lead to more questioning, to a movement that will lead us away from the structure of domination of the Roman Catholic Church toward a new Church of love, the love that has been promised us by the message of Jesus.

Roberta Imboden
Toronto, 1995

1

Introduction

If one could have been present at the gatherings where Jesus of Nazareth preached, one would have listened consistently to the images and concept of the kingdom of God, to the images and concept of love. None of us, of course, was present, but we are present now, and what do we hear being preached by the Roman Catholic Church which, supposedly, is one of the major heirs to the message of the Nazarene? We still listen to words that speak of the kingdom and of love, but something seems terribly wrong to the sensitive, informed observer. While the words still preach the Gospel of love, many of the actions of the Church, now, as well as throughout history, are not the actions of love. Individual members of the Church may have been and may be exemplars of love in the manner in which they have lived their lives, but when the Church has acted as a whole, that is, when, through the power of its hierarchy, it has acted as an institution, in most circumstances, the actions have not been those of love.

The Church, as an institution, still uses the texts of the New Testament as its preaching base. Furthermore, it has access to the findings of the skilled scriptural exegetes of the twentieth century. The problem is

1

that the message that is preached, either is distorted, or is not concretized in actions. In fact, often the actions appear to stem from some source other than the loving vision of the New Testament. Consequently, one must try to answer the question "What is wrong?" either by assuming that the answer simply lies within the Calvinistic idea that we live in a fallen world of sin and can expect nothing better, or by assuming that the answer lies within an analysis of the very structure of the Church. If ours is a fallen world, perhaps nothing can be done. But if the structure of the Church is at fault, something can be done, and the hope that was crushed toward the end of Vatican II can be revived – the hope that foresaw a true collegiality operating within the Church, a true possibility for meaningful lay participation, and a true opening to other faiths.

The thesis of this book is that hope can be revived, but that the means to this revival lie within a very careful analysis of the Church's structure and a subsequent radical restructuring process. Histories of the development of the structure of the Church have been written. Hans Küng's *The Church*[1] is the most definitive of these histories. Küng details the process whereby each of the major changes in the structure took place. Sociologists, such as Thomas O'Dea, in *The Sociology of Religion*,[2] explain, to some extent, why the elder-*episkopoi* ordination structure replaced the more free-wheeling charismatic structure of the Pauline communities. O'Dea, in turn, examines the two tendencies that occur throughout Church history, the utopian, that which is prophetic and revolutionary, and the conservative, but does not address the question, "Why does the conservative tendency dominate the Church?" He then speaks of the institutionalization of three aspects of the Church. These are: (1) the cultic aspect, (2) the aspect which concerns patterns of ideas and beliefs, and (3) the aspect which concerns forms of association or organization. The formation of a priestly caste is a part of all three aspects. Thus, the spontaneous and voluntary aspect disappears and power comes to supplant faith. "[I]nstitutionalization involves routinization, and consequently charisma is diminished" (O'Dea, 117). Diminished also is the role of the laity, for "the apostolic succession of the whole church turned more and more into the apostolic succession of a particular ministry" (Küng, *The Church*, 410). The result is that the Church can take on a transcendent, sacred quality and criticism ceases.

---

1 Küng, Hans, *The Church* (New York: Sheed and Ward, 1967).

2 O'Dea, Thomas F., *The Sociology of Religion* (Englewood Cliffs, NJ: Prentice-Hall, 1983).

But the purpose of both books is different from that of the present one. Küng's objective is to give an accurate historical account of the development of the structure of the Church, whereas O'Dea deals mainly with the effect of the institutionalization of this structure. The intent of this book is to examine the intrinsic meaning of the changes in the structure throughout the centuries and how, and ultimately why, this meaning gradually usurps the meaning of the Gospel message.

The tools that will be used to accomplish this analysis are those of Jean-Paul Sartre's *Critique of Dialectical Reason*, *Being and Nothingness*, and *Search for a Method*. His critique of the institution in *Critique of Dialectical Reason* is the foundation for all the analysis. His vision of the institution is that of a structure of domination that breaks all sovereign, free, reciprocal relationships among equals and produces in its place, through the medium of inertia, univocal impotent relationships between the authority of those in power and the remainder of the members whose only freedom and sovereignty lies within a possible memory. Later in the book, Sartrean concepts will be applied to an analysis of the development of the present structure of the Church, where the work of Hans Küng, and others, will be of particular importance for us.

But the full meaning of this development can only be seen through the interweaving of two different Sartrean theories: that of the *institution* (and the related historical category of the *group in fusion*), as developed in the *Critique of Dialectical Reason*), and that of *concrete relations*, discussed in *Being and Nothingness*. Sartre's theories of historical categories are an analysis of the relationships among individual persons as they form various groups throughout history. In fact, Sartre claims that history does not begin until persons begin to act as a group. There are several types of group: the institution, the group in fusion, the statutory group, and the organization. Sartre's concrete relations are those relationships that exist among two individual persons; these can take many forms: love, masochism, sadism, hate and indifference.

Those that are of interest here are those of love and sado-masochism. The interweaving of these two theories, something that Sartre himself did not do, produces the thesis that the structure of love is that of the group in fusion, and that of sado-masochism is that of the institution. The structures of the former are based upon equality, whereas those of the latter are based upon dominance/submission. The application of this synthesis of theory to the development of the structure of the institution of the Church, adds another dimension to the Sartrean institution theory and begins to shed light upon what throughout the ages has gradually usurped the Gospel message of love: a sado-masochistic structure.

To stress the fact that the theoretical analysis used here is not just theory, but, unfortunately, is also praxis, an historical account is given of the sadistic practices in which the institution of the Church has involved itself. These include the persecution of heretics, women and Jews during the Inquisition, the modern persecution of "critical" theologians, and the misogynistic attitudes toward women that result in a continuing apartheid system within the Church. Furthermore, the silence of the Church in the face of Hitler's final solution cannot be ignored.

Sartre's *Critique of Dialectical Reason* and *Being and Nothingness* provide the theory for the "how" concerning the usurpation and subsequent distortion of the original vision of love in the Gospels. For example, Sartre's theories lend a lucidity when examining how love and equality are lost when a certain phase of the structure of the institution falls into place, or when examining how the structure of sadism operates within the institution. But the analysis would not be complete if Sartre's theory of *deviation* and *circularity* (cf. *Critique of Dialectical Reason*, II) were not used. This aspect of his theory answers the question "why?" from a theoretical point of view. Others might answer the question from an historical point of view, as do Küng and others. For example, the historical disappearance of teachers among the Christian groups eventually led to the absorption of that charism by bishops, a situation that eventually led to a hierarchical structure. But the Sartrean theory helps to explain from a purely theoretical point of view why the original Christian message of love became distorted. Yes, it flowed through a sado-masochistic structure, but why must this structure necessarily impede the free flow of the message?

Sartre (cf. *Critique of Dialectical Reason*, II) would answer by saying that part of the explanation lies in the fact that the intentions of those who have been involved in the praxis of the Church have deviated just as much as has the objective praxis. It is through such concepts as the *practico-inert* that Sartre examines this phenomenon. If part of the problem lies in the subjective area of the human individual, and in particular within human reason, then hope emerges, and that hope lies within the sphere of dialectical reason.

For Sartre, dialectical reason can be a powerful tool for changing the world and history, since it is only dialectical reason, rather than other forms, such as analytical reason, that has the same structure as history. Analytical reason does not have the same structure as history, since history, for Sartre, is an ongoing process that flows from the past to the future, and analytical reason, unlike dialectical reason, is not part of a process or flow. Analytical reason is reason perceived in and of itself, reason removed from context, reason abstracted from all other aspects of reality, reason as pure formal structure. Analytical reason has a pristine, autonomous cast that will not allow it to be woven into the process of life which is filled with the flesh and blood of the human beings who create history. This theory of dialectical reason (developed in what is really the first section of *Critique of Dialectical Reason*, but actually is contained in *Search for a Method*) states that both dialectical reason and history have a structure that is obviously dialectical, both in a synchronic and in a diachronic way. "Synchronic" refers to a simultaneity in time, whereas "diachronic" refers to a difference in time. "Synchronic" refers to a relation that moves between two separate places within a simultaneous moment, whereas "diachronic" refers to a relation that moves back and forth between two different moments in time: present-past, present-future, etc. Within history, there is a synchronic movement that flows back and forth between various objective and subjective moments, existing within a simultaneous temporal moment, as well as a diachronic movement that flows back and forth between the present moment and the past, which that diachronic movement simultaneously preserves and transcends, and the future, which beckons, and, consequently, plays an important role in developing the present moment. Only dialectical reason shares this structure with history; therefore, only dialectical reason is truly at one with history. This oneness occurs through the mediation of *praxis*, since it is praxis that creates history, and the structure of praxis is dialectical. Praxis flows between an original external moment, through the subjective moment of reason, toward a new external moment in which the world is reordered.[3]

The ramification of Sartre's theory of dialectical reason is that only one who thinks dialectically can understand history, and, consequently, transcend the various deviations and circularities that have caused original wonderful visions to be tainted and distorted almost to the point of destruction. It is only those who think dialectically that have a hope of establishing refreshingly new ways of thinking and of living, based upon

---

3 Sartre's concept of dialectical reason does not contradict Marx's view of history, which can be labeled as the "historical dialectic." If one removes from view Engels' popularization of Marx's theory, which is usually referred to as "dialectical materialism," one sees that Marx does include the subjective element of human consciousness in the creation of human history. Marx's view, not surprisingly, is more subtle, and far more dynamic than the version of his view perpetuated by Engels. What is special to Sartre's theory is that Sartre chooses to emphasize the subjective element in a manner which would have been quite difficult for a nineteenth-century person, who, unlike Sartre, had never lived in the cultural ambiance of the psychological revolution begun by Freud.

the wisest and most loving visions that humans have ever had. Only those who think dialectically can transcend the moments of the past that have mired human beings in hopeless structures of oppression, domination, inertia and impotence and can preserve from that same past the original visions of love that were the impetus for the projects that fell into the mire of sado-masochism.

The final chapter of the book addresses the question, "What is to be Done?" Sartre's dialectical reason is its theoretical basis. If a new structure of the Church can be envisioned, it must be a structure that embodies that of dialectical reason, for only that structure can transcend the deviations of the present Church, while simultaneously preserving the original loving vision of the Christian project and remaining in touch with the movement of history. Surely, one of the basic problems of the present Church, if not *the* problem is that it has alienated itself completely from the present flow of history. The present Church reflects a medieval society that died long ago. In order to envision a new structure, this chapter turns to the one aspect of the present Church that appears to have consciously attempted to transcend the present rigidity and to explore and develop the original vision of love and justice: liberation theology. Specifically, this chapter considers Brazilian Franciscan Leonardo Boff's theory of the Trinity within the context of a Sartrean critique. Boff, himself, would like to see this theory concretized in civil society.

Thus, the analytical problem is to examine Boff's theory of the Trinity to see if its structure follows that of dialectical reason. If so, it is possible to say that a relation exists between dialectical reason and love, for at the centre of all Christian theology lies the loving God of all creation. But the analysis cannot be complete until there is also an examination of Sartre's own view of the structure of love as explained in *Being and Nothingness*. If the structure of the Trinity is seen to have the structure of Sartre's and Boff's view of love, it is possible to postulate a concrete structure for the "new" Church that would be capable of being a structure of love, of therefore being a proper vehicle for the expression of the original message of love, for it would, through its dialectical structure, be capable of transcending the sado-masochistic structure that is strangling the message of love that the present Church teaches.

While the group in fusion may embody the structure of love, the problem is that, according to Sartre, the group in fusion has proven historically to be very fleeting in duration. This group acts as a powerful tool of revolutionary change, then dissolves the moment that those changes begin to be realized. The group in fusion is, perhaps, the structure of the fulfilled kingdom, but that moment has not come. Consequently, some other form of structure must be contemplated, perhaps one based upon Boff's Trinity and Sartre's theory of the structure of dialectical reason and of his particular view of love. Some parallels, of course, should exist between the group in fusion and the new structure. The hope is that such a new structure, although lacking the perfect form of the fulfilled kingdom, would be a step toward the saving of one of the most important visions that any individual has ever had, the vision of love of Jesus of Nazareth.

2

The Inquisitions:
Sado-Masochism

The Medieval Inquisition

In order to critique the Church properly, it is necessary to begin by examining the areas that have violated what according to the New Testament is the most important of all human values: love. What actions and attitudes of the Church in history have been exceedingly unloving? To answer this question, first, we should look at the Church in the distant and more recent past. Second, we should examine the Church in the modern era, and in its post-Vatican II phase, especially under the present pope, John Paul II. Once this history is analyzed, through a Sartrean analysis of the institution, we shall see why love, the central core of the message of Jesus Christ, is incapable of being sustained within the structure of the institution of the Church – why the institution of the Church is guilty of the complete failure of love.

These areas of the blatant violation of love should not be viewed simply as unfortunate aberrations. Rather, they should be viewed as part of a continuum that extends into the daily life of the Church and of the members of that Church. For example, women no longer are imprisoned and burned for being witches, but the attitude of the Church is that women are inferior, and such a sadistic attitude, the attitude of domination, permeates the psychic state of every woman who consciously thinks of her role in the Church. Some transcend this psychic state beautifully and perform magnificent acts of love within the realm of the Church in spite of the prevailing sexist attitude, but the necessity for such transcendence is a scandal. Thus, one should view this and the following chapter as a brief examination of that part of the continuum where the message of Jesus has been most violated in a painful, public, social manner.

Historically, there have been three areas of gross violation of love: that of dissidents (usually branded "heretics"), that of the Jewish people, and that of women. The all-encompassing word for these violations is a word that everyone equates with terror: the Inquisition. Many people associate the Inquisition only with the "problem" of heresy, since, from the Church's point of view, the Inquisition rid the earth of evil heterodoxy, but heresy was defined in such broad terms that it could arbitrarily include anyone at any time: the very situation of terror.

In the present, fortunately, the Church has publicly renounced its policy of blaming the Jewish people for deicide. Pope John Paul II has renounced this policy which was in place for more than a millennia and was the foundation for European anti-Semitism. But, while former methods of torture and the ultimate punishment, burning at the stake, have receded before the slightly more genteel sensitivities of the modern world, the curial office of the Inquisition is still in place; the Congregation for the Doctrine of the Faith is its present name. The major preoccupation of this office is to search out and persecute dissidents. The world is very familiar with their names: Hans Küng, Edward Schillebeeckx, Leonardo Boff, Raymond Hunthausen, Teresa Kane, Agnes Mansour, and many others. Careers and psyches, rather than bodies, are "burned at the stake." Concerning women, the Congregation for the Doctrine of the Faith has actually sent investigators to ferret out potential problems in American convents, but it is the atmosphere of the Congregation and the attitude of the former Inquisition that still lingers within it that is so injurious to modern Catholic women. This inquisitorial attitude's most concrete form is in the well-known official Church rejection of women priests, on the grounds that no woman, because of her gender, can represent Jesus Christ, and the equally famous rejection of artificial birth control and abortion (no matter what the circumstances).

The organization and operation of the Medieval Inquisition is extremely important within the framework of attempting to highlight the more flagrant sadistic practices of the Roman Church in history, for the

Medieval Inquisition became a paradigm for the later Spanish Inquisition against the Jews and the Conversos, that is, those of Jewish origin who had converted, very often under duress, to Christianity, and the Inquisition against witches, an operation that was an important part of the phenomenon of the witch-craze of the fifteenth, sixteenth and seventeenth centuries. The Medieval Inquisition officially began in the thirteenth century. Papal legislation from 1227 to 1235, including the papal bull of Gregory IX in 1232 that stated that the secular governments were to burn heretics, established the Inquisition as a centralized institution which was staffed by Dominicans. But the papal bull *Ad extirpanda* of Innocent IV, May 15, 1252, is considered to be the official beginning of the Inquisition.

In some ways, the true beginning of the Inquisition was an action that was a violent operation that is not formally considered to be part of the Inquisition, for, at the time, the juridical procedure that was to have such a negative effect upon the next few centuries was not yet completely in place. This action was the massacre of the Albigensians in the south of France.

When the King of France refused to lead the crusade to kill the Albigensians of Languedoc in the south-east of France, Pope Innocent III made his legate, Arnaldus Amalrici, Cistercian General of Citeayx, its commander-in-chief. In his book, *The Inquisition in the Middle Ages*,[1] Henry C. Lea states that, when the Pope's army marched on Bezier, it was a massacre such as Europe had seldom, if ever, seen. Carcassonne was next. Then, Simon de Montfort, of the Fourth Crusade fame, was appointed commander-in-chief of the Pope's forces. In June of 1210, de Montfort laid siege to Minerve and when it surrendered, he ordered 140 of the Albigensians to be burned as heretics. There were no charges read out and there was no trial. All 140 were simply burned. This moment marks the first great burning of heretics in Church history and, in truth, marks the actual beginning of the Inquisition.

That Innocent III approved of de Montfort's tactics was evident at the Fourth Lateran Council in 1215 when he referred to de Montfort as "this gallant Christian gentleman."[2] Although the heresy continued, by 1230 the Albigensians of southern France were conquered. The term "Albigensians," was used in southern France to refer to people who were known in the Low Lands, Germany and Lombardy as "Catharists."

---

1 Lea, Henry Charles, *The Inquisition of the Middle Ages* (London: Eyre and Spottiswoode, 1963). Hereinafter cited as "*IMA*."

2 De Rosa, Peter, *Vicars of Christ; The Dark Side of the Papacy* (London: Bantam Press, 1988), 161.

Henceforth, I shall use the latter name in order to make clear that their group existed over quite a broad geographical area. These Catharists were so numerous in southern France that the papacy feared that the Roman Church was greatly threatened in that area.

The Catharists, of course, considered themselves to be Christians, far more than the Church of Rome whose hierarchy they denied. The Roman Church did not represent the Church of Christ and popes were not the successors of St. Peter. Instead, they were successors of Constantine. Christ rebuked worldly power, while the popes claimed it.

The Catharists also made one sacrament out of Baptism, Confirmation, Penance, and the Eucharist; they called it "Consolamentum." This sacrament, conferred by the laying on of hands, was administered only once in an individual life, except in unusual circumstances, to those who were fully instructed. These adults were then known as "perfecti." The Catharists, foreshadowing Zwingli, denied the real presence of Christ in the eucharist. Furthermore, as dualists, as neo-Manicheans, the Catharists saw matter in every form as the work of the Evil Spirit. The Devil created the material world for the purpose of entrapping the spirit. The God of the Old Testament is identified with this Evil Spirit. The God of goodness is hidden and far from this world. Christ, who was pure spirit did not really die on the cross, for his material body was an illusion. Thus, the cross is despised as the symbol of a lie. The concrete effects of this belief were that the Catharists repudiated marriage, considered procreation a sin, for it involved the entrapment of a spirit within matter and considered the Church of Rome to be the work of Satan. Foreshadowing other Protestant groups, such as Mennonites and Quakers, they denied the moral validity of capital punishment and declared the Crusaders to be murderers. Concerning the political sphere of life, they also refused the oath of fealty that was required in feudal society, and refused allegiance to princes.

But one must not leave the beliefs of the Catharists without adding that a form of dualism had been present in orthodox Christianity from the beginning. The dualism of the Persians had affected the Jews in exile and the Essenes. Then, Hellenism and the Platonic dualism that taught that matter was less real and good than spirit, became a powerful influence. By the 1140s, a mitigated dualism, exacerbating the dualism already in orthodox Christianity, appeared in southern France and along the Rhine, an attitude possibly imported by returning crusaders.[3] By

---

3   Russell, Jeffrey Burton, *Witchcraft in the Middle Ages* (Ithaca: Cornell University, 1972), 121.

1150, absolute dualists who claimed that the Devil's existence preceded the creation of the universe were in the ascendency. By 1170, helped by Bogomil missionaries from Bulgaria who came to the south of France and Italy, the absolute dualists were dominant and by the beginning of the thirteenth century the Catharist power was wide spread. The appeal was so great to all classes that the Church saw Catharism as a threat comparable to Islam.[4]

In massacring the Albigensians, the papacy put an end to open resistance to it from within the framework of European Christianity (*IMA*, 55), but there were enough Catharists remaining for the papacy to establish formally the Inquisition in 1252. Ullmann, in his preface to the 1963 edition of Lea's famous book, states:

> There is hardly one item in the whole Inquisitorial procedure that could be squared with the demands of justice; on the contrary, every one of its items was a denial of justice or a hideous caricature of it. (*IMA*, 29)

The Inquisitorial system, which did not derive its power from canon law, but rather from the pope himself, was removed from a legal framework that was operative in the episcopal courts, which were based upon the principles of Roman law, and which did have an appeal system to the papal court. Thus, the inquisitors had an authority that exceeded the authority of the bishops.

Ullmann claims that in instituting the Inquisition, the papacy was betraying its own principles of jurisprudence, principles that he claims were models for contemporary governments and subsequently influenced the development of constitutional government. Now, in the thirteenth century, the papacy was unfaithful to its own past, its past insistence upon law, justice and regularized procedure. In the ninth century, Pope Nicholas I condemned the use of torture, but in the thirteenth century Pope Innocent IV made torture part of the Inquisitorial proceedings. Principles of evidence concerning the quality of witnesses were waved aside. Whereas before the testimony of convicted perjurers, excommunicated persons, other heretics, children, servants, and spouses were banned from the court, now it was permitted.

Although one can successfully argue that the Roman Church was operating within a political and social climate that accepted and often applauded its action, it is not possible to remove responsibility from this Church, for, on the one hand, it preached the New Testament Gospel

---

4 Ibid., 122.

of love, and, on the other hand, it made certain that the secular govern-ments accepted its authority. According to papal legislation, it was the legal duty of the secular governments to exterminate heretics within their realms. In case a secular ruler did not comply with the wishes of the Inquisition, his power was threatened with the occupation of his territory by orthodox Roman Catholic princes, he himself would fall under the suspicion of heresy, and his realm would be threatened with the ecclesiastical interdict.[5]

To highlight further the fact that the Roman Church cannot be relieved of its responsibility for the Inquisition because it simply represented an age whose concept of brutality and justice was very different from ours, the Inquisition withdrew various safeguards for the accused that were part of the practice of the secular courts. The secular court gave notice in advance to the accused, who was entitled to counsel and to knowledge of the names and the testimony of witnesses. The judge was required to complete the case within thirty days. The Inquisition, on the other hand, according to Lea, was empowered to disregard forms, and to permit no impediments arising from judicial rules (*IMA*, 158). For example, Guilem Garric, an accused Catharist, was brought to a confession at Carcassonne in 1321 after having been detained in prison for thirty years (*IMA*, 172). The accused, whose guilt was assumed in advance, was allowed no counsel and was denied access to the names and testimony of the witnesses.

A common occurrence in the procedure of prosecution was the random calling of witnesses upon hearing that someone was a heretic (often the result of confession under torture) (*IMA*, 160). Furthermore, the fact that Gratian, the great encoder of canon law in the twelfth century, had for-bidden that torture be used to extract confessions, is another example of one of the forms of formerly accepted jurisprudence that was super-seded by the Inquisition. In 1252, Pope Innocent IV's bull *Ad extirpanda* ordered secular authorities "to force all captured heretics to confess and accuse their accomplices, by torture, which should not imperil life or injure limb" (*IMA*, 175). The most commonly used and "simplest" form of torture, at least at the beginning of the proceedings, was "chains and starvation in a stifling hole (*IMA*, 174). When a mass of information, composed mainly of gossip, exaggerated and distorted by the witness' fear, was finally gathered, the accused would be arrested. The names of

---

5   In England, common law was a buttress against the Inquisition. There was no secrecy attached to proceedings, no torture. There was a jury, etc.

the witnesses and the nature of the charges against the accused were withheld. The only possible means of escape was confession. Not to confess would most certainly assure that the person would be handed over to the secular arm to be burned at the stake. Not surprisingly, the overwhelming majority confessed, very often with the aid of torture, but if confession reflected true conversion, then the accused would have to betray fellow heretics. The famous French inquisitor, Bernard Gui, who was considered to be a moderate, would pardon those who voluntarily came forward and confessed and betrayed associates. Betraying a single "perfected," that is, a Catharist who had completely embraced the attitudes of that group, would insure immunity and perhaps additional reward (*IMA*, 162).

This inquisitorial procedure, needless to say, produced a climate of terror. Walter Ullmann states in his preface that there was a "virtually limitless expansion of the concept of heresy, and its ramifications into virtually every department of social and public life" (*IMA*, 27). Spies were employed. Furthermore, because of the secrecy of the inquisitorial proceedings, coupled with the casuistry practised by the highly educated and clever inquisitors, the accused persons found themselves with no means of defence. Lea claims that the inquisitors were masters in the art of confusing, of deceit and of detecting the slightest hesitancy and ambiguity (*IMA*, 164). Added to the defencelessness of the accused was the fact that Pope Innocent III embodied in canon law a decretal that, if advocates would try to aid heretics, the advocates themselves would fall under suspicion (*IMA*, 199).

There was some attempt on the part of both secular and religious authorities to restrain the abuses of the Inquisition. Philippe le Bel, Duke of Burgundy, in 1291, and Pope Clement V, in 1306, are two of the most famous examples. Philippe sent a letter to Carcassonne to seek the cessation of indiscriminate arrests, and Clement sent investigators to Carcassonne who reported that torture was habitually employed and that it was extremely severe. The Council of Vienne (1311) agreed upon reform, but Clement delayed publication of much of the legislation, and the inquisitors, having been made a law unto themselves, paid little heed.

The actual words of Bernard Gui demonstrate the extent to which the Inquisition had become a law unto itself:

> The accused are not to be condemned unless they confess or are convicted by witnesses, though not according to the ordinary laws, as in other crimes, but according to the private laws or privileges conceded to the inquisitors by the Holy See, for there is much that is peculiar to the Inquisition. (*IMA*, 185)

Unfortunately, "[i]n the administration of torture, the rules adopted by the Inquisition became those of the secular courts of Christendom at large" (*IMA*, 180). Lea claims that much that was taught by the Inquisition "found its way into general criminal law which it perverted for centuries" (*IMA*, 188).

One hears most often of the fate of those who were burned at the stake, burned by the secular authorities who were expected to perform this action under threat that they themselves would be excommunicated, and their land placed under interdict and, if this situation endured for one year, the threat could be converted into a heresy charge. But burnings occurred in the minority of cases, for that punishment was usually allotted mainly to those accused of heresy who refused to confess, and most persons confessed under torture, or to those who confessed and were later accused of relapse, but many simply died after a relatively short time in prison because of the terrible conditions.

Another large group were condemned to a life of "shunning" and of desperate poverty. These persons were required, in some cases, to wear large saffron-coloured crosses on their clothing. The Catharists also had to wear large saffron crosses on their caps. These persons were exposed to constant derision and ridicule and had great difficulty earning a living. Others were compelled to make far-flung pilgrimages that would take years, and would result in the family of the accused perishing from destitution. The non-fulfillment of a penance was dangerous. But perpetual imprisonment was the principal punishment used against those who confessed to heresy. The accused would suffer imprisonment in solitary confinement in a small, dark cell, with chains on the feet and a diet of bread and water. Sometimes the person was chained to the wall. Many died before the case had ended (*IMA*, 249). Bernard Gui's Register of Sentences, at Carcassonne, from 1308 to 1322 records 636 condemnations: 40 were burned at the stake; 300 were imprisoned; 138 were condemned to wear crosses; 16 were condemned to perform pilgrimages; the bones of 67 persons who were condemned posthumously were exhumed and burned. One person was banished to the Holy Land; thirty-six were declared to be fugitives and sixteen persons had their houses destroyed (*IMA*, 250). Confiscation of the property of the condemned was constant practice, for Pope Innocent III had proclaimed, "In the lands subject to our temporal jurisdiction we order the property of heretics to be confiscated" (*IMA*, 258). The taint of the condemned heretic fell upon the entire family of the accused and extended to the next two generations. The grandchildren, for example, could not hold public office. Frederick II began the practice, and the Roman Church adapted it to the Inquisition. Although Gui did frequently mitigate sentences, and sometimes persons were released from prison, acquittal was not part of the inquisitorial procedure, and thus, the sentence could be reimposed at any time. The slightest suspicion could reimpose the misery.

In summary, according to Lea, the greatest curse of the Inquisition, until the period of the Enlightenment, was that throughout much of Europe, the inquisitorial process, as developed for the destruction of heresy, became a paradigm for dealing with the accused: (*i*) the accused had no rights, (*ii*) guilt was assumed in advance, (*iii*) confession was extorted by guile or force, confession of both the accused and of witnesses, (*iv*) torture was also used for the purpose of obtaining the betrayal of friends, and (*v*) suspicion of a crime, in itself, constituted a crime (*IMA*, 318). "It was a system which might well seem the invention of demons, and was fitly characterized by Sir John Fortescue as the Road to Hell" (IMA, 318).

The Inquisition in Spain: the Persecution of the Jews

The Medieval Inquisition had existed in Aragon since 1238, but although it was active in France, Germany and Italy, it made only a token appearance in Aragon. Consequently, the term "the Spanish Inquisition" does not refer to that medieval period. Rather, it refers to a period that began in the fifteenth century and extended to the early nineteenth, a period that shall remain infamous for its persecution of the Jews.

The name that is associated most with this period is that of Thomas of Torquemada, a Dominican appointed as chief inquisitor of Aragon by Ferdinand on October 17, 1483. During the fifteen years of his reign of terror, 114,000 victims appeared before his inquisitorial tribunal. Of them, 10,220 were handed over to the secular authorities for burning.

Although the Inquisition was an instrument of Spanish royal policy, all authority and jurisdiction came from Rome. Furthermore, this Inquisition was based upon the Medieval Inquisition in all aspects concerning arrest, trial procedure, confiscation, etc.

One begins to see a foreshadowing of what Henry Kamen refers to as the terrifying "first twenty holocaust years" of the Spanish Inquisition[6] when one observes that the heresies that were charged against the accused by the Inquisition were no longer those of Catharism, of Waldensianism, but rather, were "heresies" of Judaism and of Islam.

---

6 Kamen, Henry, *Inquisition and Society in Spain in the Sixteenth and Seventeenth Centuries* (Bloomington: Indiana University Press, 1985), 189.

What is foreshadowed is Torquemada's campaign against Jewish heresy that began with the partial expulsion of the Jews from Spain in 1483. The total expulsion occurred in 1492, and Kamen claims that it seems that the expulsion proposal came from the Inquisition. King Ferdinand simply supported Torquemada and his organization. The reason for this expulsion of the largest Jewish community in Europe was Torquemada's desire to separate the Jews from the Conversos, those Jews who had converted to Christianity in the latter part of the fourteenth century. In 1390, Ferrant Martinez, Archdeacon of Ecaja in the south of Spain, inflamed religious fanaticism, and hundreds of Jews were murdered. In 1391, there were forced mass conversions, and it was these Conversos that Torquemada was attempting to "protect" from Judaic heresy, the "protection" taking the form of separating the Conversos from the Jewish community through the expulsion of the Jews. The expulsion was a tale of misery. After having to sell all their property, but not being allowed to receive gold or silver for it, many boarded overcrowded, ill-managed ships for North Africa, Italy and Turkey. Storms drove some back to Spain; some landed in North Africa, where they were pillaged and murdered; some were sold into servitude as men servants and maid servants in Genoa.[7]

When the Jews were expelled, the Conversos, in a sense, took their place, for they practised the same occupations: merchants, tax collectors, moneylenders, farmers, tailors and cobblers, and their communal life was very similar to that of the Jews. Thus, suspicion was cast upon all the Conversos and the Inquisition treated them as "Judaizers." It was upon these converts that the heavy hand of the Inquisition fell. But the hand of the Inquisition began to fall upon the Conversos even before the partial expulsion and the appointment of Torquemada as the inquisitor of Aragon, Valencia and Catalonia. In 1478, Pope Sixtus IV issued a bull for the appointment of two or three priests over forty years of age as inquisitors, and the chronicler Hernando del Pulgar,[8] states that the first result was that more than 4,000 families fled from Seville, Cordoba and the towns of Andalucia. Then there was an attempted armed uprising on the part of the Conversos, and after the plans were betrayed to the authorities, the leader, Diego de Susan, one of Seville's leading citizens, was burned at the stake, along with five others in February 6, 1481. According to

---

7 Ibid, 17.

8 Ibid., 30.

Andrés Bernaldez, during the first eight years of the Seville tribunal, "More than 700 persons were burnt and over 5,000 were punished."[9]

Between 1488 and 1505, 99.3 percent of the persons tried by the Barcelona tribunal were Conversos of Jewish origin. Of those tried in Valencia between 1484 and 1530, 91.6 percent were also Conversos of Jewish origin. Kamen states that "beside it the mediaeval Inquisition appears a model of moderation."[10] Hernando del Pulgar claims that by 1490 the Inquisition in Spain had burned 2,000 people at the stake. A later historian, Diego Ortiz de Zunega, stated that between 1481 and 1524 in Seville over 20,000 heretics had confessed their errors and over 1,000 were burned at the stake.[11] In Guadaloup, by 1485, nearly 40 percent of those arrested were burned; in Avila, between 1490 and 1500, nearly 41 percent of the accused were burned, and, in Valencia, 38 percent of 2,000 of the early cases ended in burning at the stake. It is estimated that three quaters of all those who perished during the 300 years of the Spanish Inquisition did so during the first twenty years. The reason for referring to the Holocaust in Spain in the latter part of the fifteenth century is now more clear.

The activity of the Inquisition against the Conversos was so severe that some of them assassinated the inquisitor of Saragossa, Pedro Arbues. But the reprisal was terrible. One of the assassins had his hands cut off. Then he was dragged to the market place where he was beheaded, and quartered. Then several pieces of his body were suspended in the streets and his hands were nailed to the door of the Deputacion. Several members of leading Aragon families were executed. Thus, open opposition to the Inquisition was ended for a hundred years.

Torture used during the Spanish Inquisition was mainly that used in the Medieval Inquisition (besides, of course, being chained and starved in one's cell). First, there was the pulley. The accused was hung by the wrists from a pulley on the ceiling. Heavy weights were attached to the feet. After the victim was raised slowly, suddenly he would be allowed to fall. The result was often that the arms and legs would be dislocated. Second, was the water torture. The accused would be tied on a rack. His mouth would be forced open and a linen cloth would be placed in his throat. Then water was slowly poured down his throat from a jar. The most common torture after the sixteenth century was to bind the ac-

---

9   Ibid., 32.

10   Ibid., 41.

11   Ibid., 41.

cused tightly on a rack by cords that were passed around the body and limbs. These cords were controlled by the executioner who would tighten them by turns of the cords. The fact that the accused was stripped simply added to the pain.

As with the descendants of the condemned of the Medieval Inquisition, the descendants of the condemned Conversos suffered greatly. According to the statutes of the "limpieza de sangre," many were barred from posts of honour and trust, and they were also barred from entering churches, colleges, convents and trade guilds.

In the eighteenth century, during the reign of Philip V, mass persecutions came to an end. Not only was Philip himself less keen to allow such an atmosphere, but heretics had been purged into extinction. Furthermore, all underground Judaism had been destroyed. But the Inquisition did not end in Spain until the nineteenth century. During the French occupation in Spain, they abolished the Inquisition on February 22, 1813. But the Inquisition did not ultimately cease to exist forever in Spain until July 1834. Growing contact with the rest of the world, namely France and the United States, was a major factor.

Unfortunately, the proceedings of the Spanish Inquisition were not the only anti-Semitic action of the Church. Paul IV, the inventor of the famous Index of forbidden books, was elected pope in May 1555. An ascetic and anti-Semite like Torquemada (a strange irony, for Torquemada himself was, at least partially, of Converso background), Paul IV shut the Jews up in ghettos. His *Cum nimis absurdum* called the Jews Christ-killers, claimed that they were by nature slaves and that they were to be confined to a particular area called, after the Venetian Foundry, a ghetto. Jews had usually lived in one particular area, but never before had they been forcibly confined to one area after their property had been confiscated and their books had been burned. The ghetto had one entrance that had a gate that would be locked at night. The Jews were forbidden to engage in commercial activity, but could sell food and second-hand clothes. They became rag-pickers. To add to their humiliation, they were required to wear yellow hats in public. Within days, other ghettos, all wretched, appeared. In the Roman ghetto four or five thousand people lived within a circuit of five hundred yards.

The Inquisition in Relation to the Witch-Craze

Parallel in time with the Spanish Inquisition, whose focus was upon Jews and Conversos, was the Inquisition against witches during the fifteenth, sixteenth and seventeenth centuries in the same areas where the Medieval Inquisition had taken place. During this period, at least 100,000 people were tortured and killed as witches.[12] By about 1450, the fear known as the witch-craze began, a fear that would last for 200 years.

One of the longest and most complex of the witch trials pitted the kings of France and England and the pope against the Templars, whose organization these authorities wished to destroy, for they feared the power of the Templars and coveted their wealth. The first accusation occurred in 1305. The Templars were accused of denying God, Christ, of desecrating the cross, of being involved in ritually obscenely kissing their prior, of adoring idols, of involvement with the Devil through intercourse with succubi and of murdering their illegitimate children. This trial was among those used as a model during the time of the later witch-craze.

According to Jeffrey Russell, as can be observed in the Templar trial and the subsequent destruction of their order, there is a definite link between the phenomenon of witchcraft, that is, its perception in the popular mind, and that of heresy, the kinds of heresy that were persecuted in the Medieval Inquisition. The charges of the Inquisition against witchcraft first appeared in the lowland countries, in France, in Germany, and the north of Italy, where heresy had been strong. It was the Dominican inquisitors under the auspices of the papacy who led these attacks in the fifteenth century, often against the resistance of local Church authorities.

The ideological link between Catharism, for example, and witchcraft, or the perception of witchcraft, was that the Catharist emphasis upon the Devil and his powers influenced orthodox theology and thus intensified the fear of the Devil. On the other hand, if indeed there were actually people who worshipped the Devil, one sees here a curious reversal of Catharism. The Catharists, as dualists, emphasized the power of the Devil because they wished to devote their lives to fighting him. Russell's theory is that in such a situation there were probably people who pondered that if the good God was hidden and remote and the Devil, who presides over wealth, fame and sex was so powerful and present, then, perhaps one should worship the Devil. A further temptation to worship the Devil could have resulted from the Catharist identification of the God of the Old Testament with the Devil, for worship of this God had been part of orthodox Christianity. Also, a belief in demons had been an element in the Judaeo-Christian religions. But whatever the situation of Devil-worshippers actually was, what was important is that the popu-

---

12 Russell, Jeffrey B., *A History of Witchcraft, Sorcerers, Heretics and Pagans* (New York: Thames and Hudson, 1980), 11.

lar imagination had been prepared through the Medieval Inquisition to invert strangely aspects of the leading heresies and to assimilate them to the concept of witchcraft.

Furthermore, the orthodox thought that the Catharists were actually wild libertines. The relationship between disgust for and an indulgence in matter had been a theme in Gnosticism, an earlier form of dualism, but no evidence, other than that which is suspect and biased, has ever shown that the majority of the Catharists were anything other than what they said they were: ascetics who lived the "perfected" life. But the belief that heretics spent much time in sexual orgies was a definite contributing factor to the witch-craze, for people simply assimilated this concept to their concept of the witch. Russell goes on to say that people projected their evil desires, passions and fears upon those who were usually the most vulnerable in society: a lonely outsider, such as old widows and old isolated women in general.[13] "The history of European witchcraft is essentially the history of a concept whose relationship to physical reality was tenuous."[14] The tragedy is that the concept caused the death of hundreds of thousands.

Other heretical groups were much closer in ideology to that of witchcraft than were the Catharists. The Antinomians, for example, taught that all action was virtuous and that Satan was God. The Luciferans, Adamites and Free Spirits heretics were very close to the concept of witchcraft. These groups advanced the spirit of rebellion against the Church, and if there actually were any real followers of witchcraft, they could be perceived to be the rebels, *par excellence.*

One again sees the mixture and the beginning of a crossover from medieval heresy to the accusation of witchcraft in a trial in 1387 in Lombardy, where the doctrines of the Catharists and the Waldensians seemed to be the ideology of the accused. But, in the course of interrogation and torture, the accused claimed that once a month they gathered in the synagogue to worship Satan, after which, of course, they all fell about in the midst of an orgy.

In the south of France, in 1438, a trial took place that, unfortunately, became a paradigm for tens of thousands of such trials. Pierre Vallin was seized by the Inquisition and repeatedly tortured. He confessed "voluntarily" to the usual crimes of witchcraft: he had invoked Beelzebub, had paid tribute to the Devil, had denied God, had desecrated the cross,

---

13 Ibid., 73.

14 Ibid., 62.

had sacrificed his own baby daughter, had gone regularly to the synagogue, had copulated with Beelzebub who had taken the form of a girl,
and had been involved in the cannibalism of the flesh of children.[15] He
was condemned, his possessions were confiscated, and he was probably burned at the stake. But as early as 1233, Pope Gregory IX accused
the Waldensians, who simply were evangelical moralists, of attending
assemblies where the Devil presided over orgies.[16]

There were both intellectual and social influences that helped to fan
the fires of the witch-craze. Scholastic theology, influenced by the struggle with the Catharist heresy, which really was introduced in the 1140s,
created a coherent intellectual structure through which the witch hunt-
ers could pursue their work. The Scholastic theologians focused upon
the pact that existed as a foundation for the ritual intercourse between
the witch and Satan. These theologians added to the concept of "orgy"
the idea of the "incubus," the demon spirit that has sexual intercourse
with women. But the fact that heretics in general were considered to
have a pact with the Devil sets the stage for the obsession with pacts
with the Devil during the witch-craze.

Another influence upon the phenomenon of witchcraft was a new
ideology of many Renaissance humanists who were neo-Platonists and
magicians, for, as neoplatonists, they held that magic could be worked
by natural means. Since the universe was united in one system, all things
were interrelated and, consequently, one could have recourse to the
supernatural without the aid of supernatural beings: it was natural magic.
But Aristotelianism really encouraged the growth in the belief in witchcraft since, unlike neoplatonism, it held that magic had to be done with
the aid of spirits.

Many social factors were, as always, a great influence in this witch-
craze climate. A time of social dislocation was at hand, a situation that
would eventually cause the authorities who had power over the status
quo to become very nervous. For example, the rapid expansion of popu-
lation, which had begun in the eleventh century, was suddenly halted
by the Black Death of 1347–49. The result was migrations to towns where
new industry and trade came into being. A restructuring of the economy
and of social institutions such as feudalism and manorialism followed.
But often older people were left behind in the countryside. In this upheaval, greater numbers of women were living alone. Russell claims that

---

15 Ibid., 78.

16 Russell, Jeffrey B., *Witchcraft in the Middle Ages* (Ithaca: Cornell University P), 126,
    160, 161.

the fact that women survived the plagues[17] more readily (by means of magic, of course), served as midwives (who became targets when infants died), worked as nurses and cooks (where, presumably, they had access to herbs that could heal, cure, or poison), contributed to the victimization of women during the witch-craze.[18]

Russell claims that women were more influential in the heretical sects, such as in the Waldensian sect, where they could serve as lay preachers, and in the Catharist where they could become "perfecti," than in orthodox Roman Christianity or in society in general where, barred from education and power, they had no influence at all. In fact, an exceptional number of women joined the Catharist sects, and one of the reasons why the Waldensians broke with the Church of Rome was that the Valdes group, a movement of apostolic poverty, was forbidden by the bishop to allow women to preach. Consequently, a great number of women were attracted to these heretical sects. But women were also attracted to orthodox, monastic and semi-monastic reform movements. The lead, often taken by women of social standing, would, undoubtedly, have disturbed the male Church authorities.[19] Again, we see the gradual assimilation of the heresy situation to that of the witch-craze, where more and more women became the accused.

But the witch-craze took on ferocious strength as the idea grew that there was a witchcraft group that was operating as a conspiracy and therefore was doubly treasonous. All heresy was seen as treason, since all heresy was perceived as being against the pope, who was perceived as the supreme authority. But witchcraft was even worse than regular heresy, since such heretics as the Catharists and the Waldensians were worshippers of God, whereas the witches were seen as worshippers of the Devil. But the greatest impetus to this new strength of the Inquisition was the appointment of Heinrich Institoris as inquisitor in the south of Germany in 1474. At first, aided by the Dominican, Jakob Sprenger, he devoted most of his investigations to accusations of witchcraft. He persuaded Pope Innocent VIII to issue the famous witch bull *Summis Desidirantes Affectibus* in 1484, and himself published the now infamous *Malleus Maleficarum*, or *The Hammer of the*

---

17 Russell, Jeffrey B., *A History of Witchcraft, Sorcerers, Heritics and Pagans* (London: Thames and Hudsor, 1980), 113–115.

18 Russell, Jeffrey B., *Witchcraft in the Middle Ages* (Ithaca: Cornell University, 1972), 280.

19 Ibid., 281.

Witches, in 1486.[20] This document had a powerful effect from the point of view of reaching many educated persons (since the printing press was now in operation), of deepening the prevailing fear of witchcraft conspiracy, and of redirecting this fear so that it fell, from now on, almost exclusively upon women. "Satyrs, Fauns (Incubi) have appeared to wanton women and have sought and obtained coition with them" (*MM*, 24). Since the Devil was usually perceived to be male, even though theologically the Devil had no gender, and since copulation with the Devil was seen to be the central aspect of witchcraft, obviously, witches must be women. The papal bull was printed as the preface to the *Malleus Maleficarum.* Thus, Innocent VIII (1484-1492) gave the papal guarantee that some women were witches and that they truly had unearthly satanic powers, especially in the realm of sex. Alexander VI (1492-1503), Julius II (1503-1513), Leo X (1513-1521) and Adrian VI (1522-1523) followed Innocent VIII in such claims.

Aside from the fact of the Devil's "maleness," women are more inclined to copulate with the Devil than are men, according to the *Malleus,* "since they are feebler both in mind and body" (*MM*, 44).

> For as regards intellect, or the understanding of spiritual things, they seem to be of a different nature from men; ... But the natural reason is that she is more carnal than a man, as is clear from her many carnal abominations. And it should be noted that there was a defect in the formation of the first woman since she was formed from a bent rib ... that is bent as it were in a contrary direction to a man. And since through this defect she is an imperfect animal, she always deceives. (*MM*, 44)

Furthermore, "through their second defect of inordinate affections and passions they search for, brood over, and inflict various vengeances, either by witchcraft, or by some other means (*MM*, 45). Woman is "more bitter than death [for] the sin which arose from woman destroys the soul by depriving it of grace ... woman is a wheedling and secret enemy" (*MM*, 47). "All witchcraft comes from carnal lust, which is in women insatiable" (*MM*, 47). Ambitious women are even more apt to "satisfy their filthy lusts" (*MM*, 47). "And blessed be the Highest Who has so far preserved the male sex from so great a crime: for since He was willing to be born and to suffer for us, therefore He has granted to men this privilege" (*MM*, 38).The flagrant, wild misogyny of the *Malleus*

---

20 Institoris (or Kramer), Heinrich and Sprenger, Joseph, *Malleus Maleficarium (The Hammer of the Witches),* trans. Montague Summers (New York: B. Blom, 1970). Hereinafter cited as "*MM.*"

Malificarum, thus, flings the passion of the Inquisition operating in the former Medieval Inquisition territory directly at women. The Spanish Inquisition, mainly because of the efforts of one of its inquisitors, deflected this craze and went its own way.

The misogyny of Heinrich Kramer (Institoris) is translated into murder when he states, "The crimes of witches, then, exceed the sins of all others ... they are not simple Heretics, but Apostates ... no matter how penitent, they must be executed" (*MM*, 77). "[V]ery little proof is required in a charge of this nature, since it takes very little argument to expose a person's guilt" (*MM*, 208). "[S]uch cases must be conducted in the simplest and most summary manner, without the arguments and contentions of advocates" (*MM*, 210). The *Malleus* certainly has to take some of the responsibility for the fact that from the fifteenth century on witches were treated more brutally than heretics, for the witches were burned upon the first conviction rather than upon relapse (MM, 70).

The *Malleus* then becomes specific about the ways in which the accused will be treated that will differ from that of the accused heretic:

(1) The accused should be shaved everywhere so that she could not conceal magical objects.
(2) The ordeal by red hot iron should be used if she refuses to confess. (*MM*, 216)

The *Malleus Malificarum*, tragically, became one of the most influential of all early printed books, and, according to Russell, simply cancelled out the moderate tradition *vis-à-vis* witchcraft within the Church, for the *Malleus*, unfortunately, was an extreme expression of an attitude that had been held for some time by the most respectable members of the Church.[21]

Russell claims that the fact that the height of the witch-craze occurs between 1560 and 1660 indicates that an important cause of this phenomenon was the rising tensions between Protestants and Catholics, tensions that culminated in the devastating Thirty Years War, 1618-1648.[22] The authorities were seeing heretical, diabolical conspiracies against their authority everywhere. At Bamberg, for example, from 1623 to 1633, Bishop Johann Georg, through the proceedings of the episcopal courts,

---

21 Russell, Jeffrey B., *A History of Witchcraft, Sorcerers, Heretics and Pagans* (London: Thames and Hudsor, 1980), 79.

22 Ibid., 83.

burned at least 600 witches. Furthermore, in France, the long medieval tradition of heresy trials had laid the foundation for the judicial repression of witchcraft.

Secular courts also held witch trials; from 1427 to 1486 the number of trials in secular courts outnumbered those in the episcopal and in the inquisitorial courts, but the Inquisition dominated the witch trials of the fifteenth century, for the theorists *vis-à-vis* witchcraft drew more upon the proceedings of the Inquisition than upon the other courts. For one thing, the records of the inquisitorial courts were more thorough. Also, the support of the papacy gave the Inquisition expanded power. The result was that, ultimately, the greatest number of witch trials did occur in areas where the Inquisition was active. This support finally caused canon law to remove witchcraft from the realm of superstition and magic and to place it in the more dangerous category of heresy. Finally, the earlier medieval heresy trials were fully assimilated to the witch trials, although no one was accused of being a Catharist or a Waldensian.

Popes, such as John XXII and his successors, Benedict XII (1334) and Gregory XI (1370-1378), encouraged the Inquisition and bishops to carry on the campaign against witches and heretics.

In summary, the Roman Church's increasing institutionalization that reached its fruition in many respects in the thirteenth century was, at that time and during the following centuries, able to exercise all of its power in a reign of terror against many groups, some of whom were obviously in revolt against this process of institutionalization. Certainly, the Catharists were in revolt, as were later such persons as Jan Hus, who was burned at the stake during the Council of Constance in the fifteenth century. Even the orthodox reform movements, such as the Fraticelli, Franciscans who preached a more ascetic life than that being lived by their order, disliked the power and wealth that was wielded by the Church. But the authorities of the Roman Church answered this revolt with brutal violence. Other groups, such as the Jews, the majority of women, and Conversos of Spain, were in revolt against no one; they were simply busy living their own lives. Thus, the overwhelming question then arises: since the Gospel of love of Jesus of Nazareth was still in existence within the Church, why did the authorities of the Church of Rome behave in such a sadistic manner? This concrete manifestation of the failure of the Gospel message of love is alarming.

3

The Inquisition of the Twentieth Century: Sado-Masochism

In 1907, Pius X issued the anti-intellectual modernism heresy-hunt, whose shadow was cast across the twentieth century until the opening of the second Vatican Council in 1962. Vigilance Committees were established that were "bound to secrecy as to their deliberations and decisions."[1]

Vatican II was to abolish the inquisitorial mode of thinking within the Catholic Church forever, but even during the Council there were ominous signs that these expectations would not be met when Paul VI began to "water down" some of the changes. Then, in 1978, with the death of Paul VI and John Paul I, when Karol Wojtyla of Poland became John Paul II, an intensification of the old inquisitorial attitudes and behaviour became more and more apparent.

---

1 Quoted in *The Church in Anguish: Has the Vatican Betrayed Vatican II?*, ed. Hans Küng and Leonard J. Swidler (San Francisco: Harper & Row, 1986), 190. Hereinafter cited as "*CA*."

This situation has led Hans Küng to assert that "The Inquisition is once again in full swing."[2] In relation to dissidents, Küng has said that this Inquisition is especially used against North American moral theologians, Central European dogmatic theologians, and Latin American and African liberation theologians. Of course, many of these persons would not even consider themselves to be dissidents, but the Vatican does.

Although the torture chambers are now closed and auto-da-fé is outlawed by secular governments which now have greater power, the form, if not the content, of the old Inquisition remains, and, according to Küng, careers and psyches are destroyed. In Holland and Switzerland, whole episcopates are invited to Rome for a "closed session" in relation to some course of action that they have followed of which Rome disapproves. The "closed session" is the form of the old Inquisition whose entire mode of action during a "trial" was secrecy. Furthermore, the most secret archive of Inquisitorial authority still remains totally closed (*CA*, 61).

The most famous theologians who have recently been the victims of the twentieth-century Inquisition are, of course, Hans Küng, Edward Schillebeeckx, Leonardo Boff, and Charles Curran. There have been others, including Karl Rahner, the most outstanding Catholic theologian of the twentieth century, but these cases, explained briefly, will confirm the fact that the form of the old Inquisition is still operative, although the content of its workings is less brutal.

In 1957, Dossier 399/57/i was begun in Rome on Hans Küng when he published his doctoral thesis. In 1968, after the Church proceedings against his 1962 book *Structure of the Church* ended happily, Küng was called before the Congregation for the Doctrine of the Faith in relation to his book, *The Church*. Later, yet another of his books, *Infallible?: An Inquiry*, came under investigation, and, on February 5, 1975, the Vatican told him not to advocate his ideas on infallibility. On December 18, 1979, the Vatican declared that Küng "can no longer be considered a Catholic theologian or function as such in a teaching role."[3] The consequence was to be that, on the basis of a concordat between the Vatican and Hitler's Germany in 1933, Küng would be replaced as professor of Catholic theology at the University of Tübingen through the request of the local Catholic bishop. Fortunately, the Vatican's attempt to destroy his career

---

2 Küng, Hans, "Cardinal Ratzinger, Pope Wojtyla and the Fear at the Vatican: An Open Word After a Long Silence," in *CA*, 68.

3 Quoted in Leonard Swidler, "A Continuous Controversy: Küng in Conflict," in *CA*, 198.

was not successful, for, although he was removed from his post, thanks to the intercession of secular authorities, he remains professor of ecumenical theology and director of the ecumenical institute at the University of Tübingen and is permitted to sit on doctoral committees in the Catholic theology faculty. But to this day Küng has never been permitted to see his dossier.

The case of Edward Schillebeeckx involves not only this theologian, but also the entire Dutch Church, which, until recently, was one of the most progressive of all of the Catholic churches. As in the case of Hans Küng and his famous critique of the doctrine of the infallibility of the pope, the Church saw Schillebeeckx's theology, especially his hermeneutical method, as a threat to its authority, for Roman officials feared that this method would relativize the central authority of the Church. As we shall see also in the case of Leonardo Boff, it is usually the perception of threat that causes the central authority of the Church to move into its inquisitorial mode.

On December 24, 1960, a Dutch pastoral letter, which Schillebeeckx had helped to prepare, stated that the central Church authority was situated within and not above the Church community. In 1962, the Italian translation was withdrawn, and, in 1968, *Le Monde* made public the threat of official Roman proceedings against Schillebeeckx. The September 24, 1968 edition of *Le Monde* reported that the Congregation of the Doctrine of the Faith suspected Schillebeeckx of heresy and was initiating proceedings. Besides a seemingly unacceptable interpretation concerning revelation, the Congregation was not sympathetic with Schillebeeckx's optimistic attitude toward secularization. Karl Rahner defended him at the Vatican on October 7, 1968.

But in 1974 another official investigation was under way. This time Schillebeeckx's hermeneutical method was analyzing the historical Jesus in response to Rudolf Augstein's book, *Jesus, the Son of Man*. The letter that Schillebeeckx received from the Congregation of the Faith asked a very revealing question: "Can you give an unambiguous reassuring explanation regarding the hierarchic structure of the Church?"[4] On July 6, 1978, the Congregation requested that Schillebeeckx come to Rome personally. They were concerned about his attitude toward the normative character of ecumenical councils, the infallible teaching authority of the pope, and Jesus and the founding of the Church. Four

---

4 Quoted in Ad Willems, "The Endless Case of Edward Schillebeeckx," in *CA*, 216.

months after the death of Paul VI, on December 13, 1979, a "conversation" began, but the Nimegen exegete, Professor Bas van Iersel, saw the conversation as a "judicial hearing" (*CA*, 217). The hearing concerned what appears to be at the core of the Vatican's state of tension with the entire Western world, in general, and Catholic theologians, in particular. The Vatican believes in "eternal unchangeable truth," and Schillebeeckx, a modern person influenced by the historical critical method, rejects the notion "that there exists a truth in 'itself,' that would be palpable in its unchangeableness. The unchangeable truth is attained in hermeneutical translation, in the interpretation of the ecclesial community" (*CA*, 218). As in medieval inquisitorial hearings, there was no acquittal, even though there was no ultimate condemnation.

The fact of non-acquittal became quite apparent when in 1982 a commission of Dutch and Flemish Dominicans were requested to investigate Schillebeeckx's latest book. At the core of the problem again was the central authority of the Church. Schillebeeckx thought that the Church's concept of apostolicity was too narrowly defined. Whereas the Vatican insists that whether a particular Christian community has apostolicity depends upon whether an ordained priest is present, Schillebeeckx feels that apostolicity has an inner dimension, as well as a juridical one. For him, if the faith community preserves in its teachings and actions the teachings and actions of the apostles, that is, the desire to follow and to be like Jesus, then, even though no ordained priest is present, this community has apostolicity.

Subsequently, Schillebeeckx was summoned to Rome. He went to Rome on July 24, 1984. But this event did not cease the investigations. The very next year, the Vatican mobilized itself again in relation to Schillebeeckx' 1985 book, *The Church with a Human Face*, which advocated some change in the canon law of 1983, the reorganization of the diaconate and the establishment of a fourth order beyond the present priesthood.[5]

Harvey Cox, in his book, *The Silencing of Leonardo Boff*, states that the power that Jesus uses is the power to love and that he warned his disciples:

> You know that among the Gentiles the recognized rulers lord it over their subjects and the great make their authority felt. It shall not be so with you; among you whoever wants to be great must be your servant. (Mark 10: 42-43)

5 Schillebeeckx, Edward, *The Church with a Human Face: A New Expanded Theology of Ministry* (London: SCM, 1985).

Boff claims that when Jesus said, "Full authority in heaven and on earth has been committed to me" (Matt. 28:18) and then passed this power on to the apostles, that "it was not *potestas*, the power to dominate and rule, but an astounding power to be patient and to support even ingrates and evil doers."[6] Boff says that the power of love is different in nature from the power of domination; it is fragile, vulnerable, conquering through its weakness and its capacity for giving and forgiveness. Unfortunately, *potestas* became the prevailing form of power within the Church. Boff's attitude, expressed in his *Charism and Power,* sent the machinations of the Congregation of the Doctrine of Faith against him – an action that ironically proved Boff's point.

Of course, Boff's strong affirmation of liberation theology and the "base communities"[7] from which it has sprung was very much behind the Vatican's move against him. After Medellin, when priests and nuns began to live and to work in the slums, the Gospels, seen through the prism of liberation theology, became the model. And now we see a relationship with the Vatican's displeasure with Schillebeeckx, for the priests worked with local lay organizations. Herein lies the crux of Boff's point about *potestas*: the priests encouraged lay-administered base communities. Such a movement would increase the power of Jesus, of love, and would decrease the *potestas* of the central authority of the Vatican.

Cardinal Ratzinger, formerly the bishop of Munich and chosen personally for the task of heading the office of the Congregation of the Doctrine of faith by John Paul II in 1979, issued a famous book, in 1985, called *The Ratzinger Report on the Faith,* in which he reveals an attitude that is opposite to that of Boff. Whereas Boff is delighted with the recent

---

6 Cox, Harvey, *The Silencing of Leonardo Boff: The Vatican and the Future of World Christianity* (Oak Park, Ill.: Meyer Stone Books, 1988), 50, 51.

7 Base communities ("*communidades de base*" in Portuguese): Liberation Theology is the theoretical expression of the new form of Christianity that was being practised in Brazil, and then spread throughout Latin America in the 1960s. In the various slums of Brazil, small groups of people would meet to discuss the Gospels. The diminishing number of priests in Latin America meant that these groups were usually made up of the laity. A priest was sometimes present, but never acted as leader, only as advisor and facilitator. Discussions of the Gospels involved a powerful political dimension which the people applied to their own lives. My personal encounters with these groups in Brazil and in Nicaragua, and my length discussions with Liberation Theology priests, especially those who have lived among these communities througout Latin America (and in Africa, for these communities now flourish there), point to the conclusion that these base communities are examples of Sartre's "group in fusion." These groups are radically democratic: no form of hierarchy is present; they are love communites.

changes in the world of Catholicism, such as the base communities in
Latin America, and particularly in his native Brazil, Ratzinger assesses
the state of the Church and Christianity since Vatican II in the darkest
tones. He sees only "self-destruction," and "a progressive process of decadence" because of "the unleashing within the Church of latent polemical
and centrifugal forces." Moreover, he sees the Church in "confrontation
with a cultural revolution in the West" that he obviously regards as "self-
destructi[ve]" and decadent.[8] Ratzinger wants "re-centrage," whereas Boff
wants "de-centrage," so that the Gospel can flourish in a variety of cul-
tures. The final result of this difference was that the Congregation of the
Doctrine of the Faith silenced Boff on May 9, 1985.

In May, 1984, Boff received a six-page letter from Ratzinger, via Friar
John Vaugn, stating several objections that he had to his book *Charism
and Power*. These objections concerned Boff's theological method, his
ideas concerning the structure of the Church, his concepts concerning
dogma and revelation and the exercise of sacral power. Ratzinger then
asked for a "colloquy" with Boff in Rome within the next couple of
months. Boff wrote back and asked: (1) that the colloquy be held in Brazil, and (2) that it be held in cooperation with the Brazilian Bishops Commission on Doctrine whose president is Cardinal Aloisio Lorsheider. On
June 16, Ratzinger replied that the colloquy would take place only between the two of them in Rome, with only one other person present, a
person chosen by Ratzinger. The inquisitorial form appears: no defence
or witnesses for the accused. Also, the dismissal of collegiality with the
Brazilian bishops and the consequence of recentrage under Vatican power
is obvious. Cardinal Lorsheider personally disagreed with Ratzinger and
personally asked that he be present at the "colloquy," which was now
called an "interrogation," but Ratzinger claimed that canon law did not
call for it and that he did not want to create an undesirable precedent.

On the morning of September 7, while preparing to go to the office of
the Congregation of the Doctrine of Faith, Boff asked that the Franciscan
(Boff's order) minister general be allowed to accompany him to the outer
gate of the Congregation's headquarters and that some Franciscans be allowed to accompany him in the car en route. Both requests were denied.

Harvey Cox claims that Ratzinger's remarks during the meeting, at
which only Ratzinger and Boff were present, seemed to imply that, if
one accepted Boff's ideas,

---

8 Cox, Harvey, *The Silencing of Leonardo Boff: The Vatican and the Future of World
   Christianity* (Oak Park, Ill.: Meyer Stone Books, 1988), 79.

then some expressions and manifestations of the Roman Catholic church might not be seen as carrying the full presence of the church of Christ.... The hierarchy, or parts of it? The content of certain of the papal teachings or those of colleges of bishops? The sacred Congregation for the Doctrine of the Faith?[9]

Then the second section of the interrogation began and, accompanied by another officer of the Congregation, Cardinals Aloisio Lorscheider and Paulo Evaristo Arns of São Paulo arrived. Their request had finally been granted.

When Boff and the cardinals returned to Brazil, they thought that the affair was over; however, in March,1985, Boff received a Letter of Notification from Ratzinger, stating that he was going to make public the doctrinal elements in the six-page letter that the cardinal had sent him nearly a year earlier. Boff responded humbly, but on May 9 the notice from Rome ordering his silencing arrived. Boff could continue to say mass and could teach the handful of Franciscan students who were studying at his monastery, but he would have to forego publishing anything, stop his editing work at "Vozes," and avoid all public appearances or contact with the press. Boff and the liberation theology that he represented had received public chastisement from the Vatican.

Eleven months later, after several Brazilian bishops had an audience with the Pope concerning Boff, the silence was lifted. Cox claims that "nearly everyone in Brazil knew full well that someone in Rome, presumably the pope himself, had wanted the silence lifted before the 400 Brazilian bishops gathered in mid-April for their annual assembly."[10]

Nevertheless, as with Schillebeeckx, Boff's harassment is a continuing affair. A few months after his *Trinity and Society* was published, Cardinal Sales of Rio de Janeiro announced that the diocesan Commission for the Doctrine of the Faith was examining the book *And the Church Became People*. This book, which places the primacy of community before that of hierarchy and praises the base communities as a new form of church, was explicitly condemned by John Paul II.

Since John Paul II's and Ratzinger's view of liberation, as well as of the Church structure, is radically different from that of Boff and of the other liberation theologians, this inquisitional problem will continue. The Pope and Ratzinger see liberation only in a transcendental aspect that lies beyond life and death, whereas Boff and the

---

9 Ibid., 99, 100.

10 Ibid., 113.

other liberation theologians see it as an historical process. Liberation takes place in this world.

The long arm of the Inquisition touched theologians in the United States when, in August 1986, Ratzinger barred Charles Curran from teaching at a Catholic university. The Congregation of the Doctrine of the Faith was condemning Curran's teachings on the indissolubility of marriage, abortion, euthanasia, masturbation, artificial conception, premarital intercourse and homosexual acts. Thus, Curran was removed from his teaching post at Catholic University in Washington, D.C. The punishment dealt to Curran was essentially that dealt to Hans Küng.

Since July 1979, the Vatican had been conducting formal investigations into Curran's teachings. The 1986 condemnation occurred after a "concluding conversation" between Curran and the three highest officials of the Congregation of the Doctrine of the Faith.[11]

For the first time (and to a very harsh degree), the Congregation of the Doctrine of the Faith applied Canon 1371 of the new 1983 Canon Law. The canon states:

> The following are to be punished with a just penalty ... a person who pertinaciously rejects the doctrine mentioned in Canon 752 who does not make a retraction after having been admonished by the Apostolic See or by the ordinary.[12]

Canon 752 reads:

> A religious respect of intellect and will, even if not the assent of faith, is to be paid to the teaching which the Supreme Pontiff or the college of bishops enunciate on faith or morals when they exercise the authentic magisterium even if they do not intend to proclaim it a definitive act; therefore, the Christian faithful are to take care to avoid whatever is not in harmony with that teaching.

Thus, freedom of thought for a theologian means teaching exactly what the pope says that one may teach. Not to do so means the destruction of one's career.

---

11 Quoted in Bernard Häring, "The Curran Case: Conflict between Rome and the Moral Theologian," in *CA*, 235.

12 *The Code of Canon Law: A Text and Commentary*, ed. James A. Coriden et al. (New York: Paulist Press, 1985).

The Inquisition of the Twentieth Century: The Jews

Although the Church in the twentieth century has not continued its earlier persecution of the Jews,[13] the silence of the papacy during World War II *vis-à-vis* the deportation and subsequent massacre of European Jewery is a crime of omission that bears the silent mark of Torquemada. The Vatican did chastize the Nazis in the 1937 encyclical "With Burning Concern" when it feared the pseudo-biological basis of racism would interfere with Church authority. Michael Marrus asserts:

> The tendency of fascist movements, especially Nazism, to use race as a foundation of their regimes directly challenged the church's claims in the fields of baptism, marriage, and, more broadly, the definition of who was and who was not a Catholic.[14]

Nevertheless, in 1941, when Leon Berard, French ambassador to the Holy See, sent a letter to his Vichy government, he noted that the Vatican showed little interest in Vichy's anti-semitic laws, and worried only that they might interfere with Church juisdiction, or involve breaches of "justice and charity."[15]

> Church officials may have been the first to pass on to the Holy See sinister reports about the significance of deportation convoys in 1942, and they continued to receive the most detailed information about mass murder in the east.[16]

Diplomatic channels and other contacts, which had informed the Vatican when the mass killings began, continued to keep the Vatican well informed. But, in spite of appeals, Pope Pius XII, following his policy of neutrality, made no direct denunciations of the murder of Jews and no attempt to demand that the Nazis stop the killing. In the autumn of 1943, under German occupation, Jews were rounded up all over Rome, but the pope said nothing. It was undoubtedly this silence that caused the German ambassador, Ernst von Weisecker, to report to Berlin that the pope was pro-German. Some have said that Weisecker was protecting the pope; others have said that the ambassador was reporting the truth.

---

13 John Paul II has said recently, "To this day, Auschwitz does not cease to admonish, reminding us that anti-Semitism is a great sin against humanity." *Crossing the Threshold of Hope*, ed. Vittorio Messori (Toronto: Alfred A. Knopf, 1994), 97.

14 Marrus, Michael R., *The Holocaust in History* (London: Penguin Books, 1987), 180.

15 Ibid., 180.

16 Ibid., 180.

According to Leon Papeleux, the policy of the Vatican, like that of other neutrals, shifted, but the pope remained very reluctant to speak, and then, only weakly, toward the end of the war. Some papal nuncios, such as those in Bucharest, in Budapest, and in Turkey, the future John XXIII, were very openly sensitive to the Jewish tragedy. But Pope Pius XII, the official head of the Church, appeared to value the life of the institution over which he ruled far more than the lives of European Jewery. The existence of the institution of the Church became the supreme value.

The Inquisition of the Twentieth Century: Women

In describing the Church's attitude to women, such phrases as "patriarchal domination," "sexual repression," and "moral terrorism" come to the lips of such modern theologians as Rosemary Radford Ruether and Madonna Kolblenschlag. Kolblenschlag has claimed that the moral terrorism began in 1979, and Ruether has spoken of the personal misogyny of John Paul II.[17]

Perhaps one of first manifestations of this attitude was symbolically displayed during John Paul II's 1979 visit to the United States. When he celebrated the eucharist on the mall in Washington, D.C., he forbade women to serve as ministers of the eucharist at the celebration. When the Jesuit, William Callahan, organized a protest, he was removed from his post in Washington. Not surprisingly, the crowd at the eucharist was much smaller than had been expected.

When in 1983 Ratzinger appointed the Jesuit, Terry Sweeney, as Prefect of the Congregation of the Doctrine of the Faith, Sweeney, a sociologist, developed a questionnaire for American bishops concerning so many of the matters that directly affect women: contraception, women priests, divorce, abortion, married clergy, and homosexuality. The results of the questionnaire showed that the views of large numbers of American bishops differed from those of the Vatican. Consequently, Sweeney was asked to destroy the results. When he refused, he was dismissed from the Jesuits. The twentieth century did not bode well for women in relation to the Catholic Church when, in the early decades, the Vatican and American bishops opposed women's suffrage. Many decades later, the American Catholic hierarchy did not endorse the Equal Rights Amendment.

----

17   Ruether, Rosemary Radford, "John Paul II and the Growing Alienation of Women from the Church," in *CA*, 282.

According to Reuther, this general misogyny, and, in particular, the misogyny of John Paul II, has caused Catholic women to feel disaffected and women in general to see Catholicism as an agent of evil rather than of good. Perhaps the pope's "patriarchal anthropology" (*CA*, 281) is the most disquieting aspect of this evil. This anthropology has made the pope deduce that maleness was essential to Christ. The consequence of this deduction is that women are not allowed to be ordained, for they cannot possibly represent Christ. Reuther, along with other theologians, says that such an anthropology would make questionable whether or not women are represented or redeemed by Christ. Although it was Paul VI in 1976 who made the proclamation concerning women's inability to represent Christ, John Paul II has repeated this stance.

In the early 1980s, Mercy sister Theresa Kane, president of the U.S. Leadership Conference of Women Religious, fought strongly for a greater role for women in the ministry of the Church. But when she raised the issue with the pope on his visit to the United States, her words fell upon deaf ears.

Hans Küng has stated that the pope is "leading an almost unbelievable battle against those modern women who are seeking a life-style that corresponds to the times." He adds that "the women's question will increasingly become the test case of this pontificate."[18] Küng is obviously referring to all of the basic issues of the time that apply fundamentally to the health and welfare of women and to their future, that is, artificial birth control and abortion.

The inquisitorial mode of the Vatican displayed itself clearly in relation to this sort of issue in the case of Agnes Mansour. After thirty years of commitment to religious vows and community as a sister of Mercy, Agnes Mansour and two other sisters of Mercy, Teresa Kane and Elizabeth Morancy, were ordered to be dismissed from their communities by the Vatican (*CA* 254–255). According to Madonna Koblenschlag, there was no sense of fairness in the proceedings. The Congregation of the Doctrine of the Faith, again completely disregarding any form of collegiality, overrode the objections of all of the women's religious superiors and refused them the possibility of canonical appeal. Again, inquisitorial procedure. Not only was the Vatican placing itself in a poor light *vis-à-vis* the secular law of the leading countries of the modern world, but also, it placed itself in a poor light with regard to its own law.

---

18 Küng, Hans, "Cardinal Ratzinger, Pope Wojtyla and Fear at the Vatican: An Open Word After a Long Silence," in *CA*, 69.

The Vatican cancelled its own canon law through its prohibition of the three sisters being re-admitted to orders. Such arbitrariness is part of the moral terror of which Kolblenschlag speaks.

A few weeks later, the Vatican Sacred Congregation for Religious and Secular Institutes issued a draft on "The Essential Elements in the Church's Teaching on Religious Life" (demanding that religious return to the lifestyle and theology of pre-Vatican II), accompanied by a pastoral letter from John Paul II addressed to the bishops of the United States, asking them to conduct a pastoral investigation of religious (women's) orders in the United States.[19] Archbishop John Quinn was to head the investigation and to report to Rome. Only the religious communities of the United States were under investigation.

This new inquisitorial mode only exacerbated the thoughts and feelings of the U.S. women, some of whom, among the sisters of Mercy, had recently had to take a "loyalty oath" in relation to a slanderous article in the *Catholic Register* in November 1979 written by a Rev. William Smith concerning the fact that a "leadership group" in Teresa Kane's community was advocating direct sterilization procedures in the Mercy hospitals. Rome still was suspicious of these women who perhaps had not completely submitted their "'hearts and minds' to the magisterium" (*CA*, 253–254). Koblenschlag points out that the Vatican was acting upon the advice and information, or misinformation, of right-wing elements in the Church in the United States. One should add here that Rome was exceedingly receptive to these right-wing elements.

Archbishop Quinn was considered to be quite fair in his proceedings, but a feeling of persecution hangs in the air over the U.S. religious communities, for in his message to the U.S. conference of bishops, John Paul II urged them "to exercise their pastoral mission to religious women in accordance with the 'Essential Elements'"(*CA*, 256). Thus, a group of men in the U.S. hierarchy, directed by a man, John Paul II, were attempting to drag back to the Tridentine Church of the past 500 years a group of women who some sociologists have described as "the largest single group of educated, articulate, bonded women the world had ever seen" (*CA*, 251).

In 1984, the famous *New York Times* advertisement that grew out of the election campaign and candidacy of Geraldine Ferraro, concerning the fact that there is a diversity of opinion in the Catholic community in relation to non-infallible moral teachings, received a strong response

---

19 Kolbenschlag, Madonna, "John Paul II, U.S. Women Religious, and the Saturnian Complex," in *CA*, 255.

from Rome, in spite of the fact that it did not ask for Catholic approval of abortion. It only asked for the right to discuss the issue within the Catholic Church. The Vatican stated that the sisters who had signed the advertisement would be dismissed from their orders unless they recanted. This time, sisters received support from their superiors and refused to recant. The result: emissaries were sent from Rome for "dialogue" (*CA*, 256). Ultimately, all but two of the sisters were "cleared," but the overall result was the feeling of the massive domination of Rome and the powerlessness of U.S. women religious.

A concrete sense of the fact that the powerlessness of these religious women is a very real aspect of objective reality was manifested during the process of revising the constitutions of the religious orders, a process mandated by Vatican II. Many disagreements occurred between the U.S. women and Rome concerning "the understanding of authority and obedience, nonhierarchical structures of governance, and appropriate cultural expressions of their way of life" (*CA*, 257). Many of these constitutions were returned, with the inclusion of a vow of absolute obedience to the papacy. Never before in history had such an explicit request for an oath of obedience been demanded of these religious communities. All of these loyalty and obedience vows have the ring of a mentality of McCarthyism, the mark of the inquisitorial mind.[20]

Added to this atmosphere of oppression of U.S. religious women is the fact that women, as teachers, directors, etc., have been purged from Catholic seminaries in the midst of warnings about "secular feminism" and "'dangerous' feminist scholarship" by the U.S. National Conference of Catholic Bishops (*CA*, 257). On October 16, 1986, *Origins* published a document, released on October 5, 1986, to U.S. Catholic bishops by Cardinal William W. Baum, prefect of the Vatican Congregation for Catholic Education. It was quite explicit in excluding women and the "Great Unordained" in general.[21] Arlene Anderson Swidler makes some very interesting comments concerning this exclusion. One rector of a seminary complained that the exclusion would cause a real deficiency in the training of these seminarians. For example, Swidler says, moral teaching has always stressed the sin of pride, but pride is not at all the problem for women that it is for many men (*CA*, 292). Consequently, the inclusion of women as teachers is important, for they can bring a

---

20 Arthur Miller recognized the relationship between McCarthyism and "witch burning" in his play *The Crucible*.

21 Swidler, Arlene Anderson, "Women and the Seminaries," in *CA*, 291.

dimension of spirituality and an understanding of spiritual life that was formerly lacking. One can also only stand aside in horror at the thought that since all women and all lay men, including, of course, married men, will be excluded, male seminarians will be taught in an exclusively male clerical environment where, for the most part, the exclusively traditional male clerical celibate point of view will be exercised on such issues as artificial birth control, abortion, marriage and divorce.

The foregoing summary of some notable forms of sadistic Church praxis is intended to highlight the Roman Church's failure to live the praxis of love, the love that was the vision of Jesus. This failure manifested itself in the Medieval Inquisition, in the Spanish Inquisition and in the inquisition against women, as some of the most sadistic praxis experienced in the Western world. In more recent times, this sadistic praxis has been far more subtle. Flesh is no longer allowed to be burned at the stake, and, although Amnesty International tells of various forms of torture taking place in the world, the Church is held in check by the more progressive societies that forbid such praxis. But the Church is still capable of torturing minds and souls, of ruining lives, careers and relationships.

In 1989, the Vatican promulgated a new fidelity oath. Theologians no longer have the right to dissent publicly from official church teachings, whether or not those teachings are considered infallible or are explicitly based on divine revelation. Also, in the late spring of 1990, in the United States, Cardinal O'Connor of New York threatened any Roman Catholic politician running for public office with excommunication if that politician publicly supported a woman's right to procure an abortion. Exactly why this failure of love occurs and why sadism continues to be part of Church praxis are the next questions to be analyzed.

4

Sartrean Analysis of the Church's Failure of Love

The recognition that these varying forms of Inquisition against dissidents, Jews and women throughout the centuries are the most flagrant forms of the failure of love within the Roman Catholic Church in history is the first step. The second necessary step is to understand that the very structure of the Church is at the core of this failure. It is here that two of Jean-Paul Sartre's major works, *Being and Nothingness*[1] and *Critique of Dialectical Reason*[2] become very important.

In *Being and Nothingness,* Sartre explores the various types of relationships that can exist between human persons. He speaks of love, masochism, indifference, desire, hate and sadism, but the concrete relations that are pertinent to this analysis are love, masochism and sadism. In *Critique of Dialectical Reason,* Sartre leaves behind, seemingly, the personal

---

1 Sartre, Jean-Paul, *Being and Nothingness*, trans. Hazel E. Barnes (New York: Simon and Schuster, 1978); hereinafter cited as "*BN.*"

2 Sartre, Jean-Paul, *Critique of Dialectical Reason*, trans. Alan Sheridan-Smith (London: New Left Books, 1976); hereinafter cited as "*CDR*, II."

world of concrete relations and analyses what he refers to as "historical categories," that is, the various human formations that make up history. Here he lists the "group in fusion," the "statutory-pledged group" (really, the second phase of the group in fusion), the "organization" and the "institution," but for this analysis we shall explore only the group in fusion (and its statutory phase) and the institution. Although Sartre himself never weaves together the concrete relations of his *Being and Nothingness* and the historical categories of his *Critique of Dialectical Reason*, if one pursues the notion of the interfacing of these two aspects of his thought, it is possible to attain some interesting insights. One is that the form that love takes once it moves from the personal to the societal level is that of the "group in fusion." On the other hand, the form that masochism and sadism take when they move onto the societal level is the "institution." In other words, the group in fusion is the concrete, historical embodiment of love in history, whereas the structure of the institution is the embodiment of sado-masochism in history. Since, for Sartre, sado-masochism ultimately results from the failure of love, we can conclude that, because the Church has become a highly structured institution, perhaps the cause of its dramatic failure of love is the very structure of the Church itself. To pursue this line of analysis more carefully, however, Sartre's concrete relations and historical categories need to be examined rather closely.

For Sartre, in his *Being and Nothingness*, the first real situation of potential concrete relations with others begins with the Look: the Other looks at me. But this seemingly simple action is fraught with profound meaning. This look founds my being, causes me to be possessed by the Other, for "the Other holds a secret – the secret of what I am" (*BN*, 475). The Other confers upon me the being, the in-itself, the pure matter (that I view as that which is not the conscious me) that I am fleeing. But since it is I alone who am responsible for my being-for-others, my fundamental project becomes the recovery of my being that the look has stolen from me. I want to found my own being, to cease to be the object for the Other that the look has caused me to become.

For Sartre, there are two possible attitudes that we can have in relation to the Other and the subsequent Look. Either we transcend the Other's transcendence that threatens our freedom or we attempt to incorporate that transcendence within ourselves "without removing from it its character as transcendence" (*BN*, 474). This latter attitude involves the acceptance of being-looked-at. It is in the concrete relation of love that we try to incorporate that transcendence within ourselves.

What transpires in the situation of love is that I, the lover, demand that I become the whole world for the beloved, a world in which he must lose his freedom. In that sense, I become a special sort of object. I ask the beloved to accept me as "the unsurpassable," "the absolute end," "an absolute totality" (*BN*, 482), the source of all values, the absolute value which he can never transcend, the chosen foundation of his transcendence and the objective limit of his freedom. My independence is then assured. I am an "object-transcendence" (*BN*, 481) for the Other. "The Other's look no longer paralyzes me with finitude" (*BN*, 482). What the beloved does for me through his freedom is to found my essence, and in accepting my demand, as far as this particular relationship is concerned, prevents me from being an object that the beloved can transcend. Thus, the primary project *vis-à-vis* others in the world, to recover one's being and freedom, is accomplished in the most human manner.

The lover must maintain the subjectivity of the beloved, for the moment that the beloved becomes an object, the spell is broken and love collapses. The Other must maintain subjectivity in order for me to identify with his freedom. But I must remain an object to him, for my ideal is always to be other to myself, for "it is this being-as-object which alone can serve me as an instrument to effect my assimilation of the other freedom"(*BN*, 476). I long "to be identified with the Other's freedom" (*BN*, 476), to be other to myself, a situation which is the goal, the ideal, the purpose, of my relationship with the Other. My relations with others are always haunted by a desire for me to found my own being, to give to myself freely my being-in-itself as other. In that situation, I would become "the very being of the ontological proof – that is, God" (*BN*, 476).[3]

Sartre makes clear that the demand of the lover for pure engagement can never be fulfilled totally. The reason lies primarily in the fact that "consciousnesses are separated by an insurmountable nothingness, a nothingness which is both the internal negation of the one by the other and a factual nothingness between the two internal negations" (*BN*, 489, 490). Love attempts, in a contradictory effort, "to surmount the factual negation while preserving the internal negation" (*BN*, 490). Also, the lover could not absorb the freedom of the Other as other if this original contradiction were overcome. Furthermore, since my project as lover is to "interiorize the whole system" (*BN*, 484), that is, since my project includes the beloved's founding my being and my assimilating his freedom, conflict will occur, for my project is to be my own foundation.

Not surprisingly, Sartre sees the situation of love as being one of conflict, for the fact of the Other's freedom founding my being places me in

---

3 The absolute-being, God, is the one who is both for-itself and in-itself; it is "other as itself" and "freely giv(es) to itself its being-itself as other"(*BN*, 476). God is the one who creates "himself."

a state of insecurity. I must "get hold of this freedom and reduce it to being a freedom subject to my freedom" (*BN*, 477). But the lover does not wish to act upon the Other's freedom; the lover wishes "to exist a priori as the objective limit of [the beloved's] freedom" (*BN*, 479). I desire to possess the beloved's "freedom as freedom" (*BN*, 478); to possess the beloved as a thing is to destroy love. Thus, the lover demands a pledge. The lover wants the beloved to vow freely that the lover will be the object-limit of his transcendence. The lover wants "the Other's freedom [to] determine itself to become love" (*BN*, 479). Sartre speaks of a captivity "that is both free and yet chained in our hands" (*BN*, 479).[4]

In *Critique of Dialectical Reason*, Sartre explains that the moment that determines when the group in fusion is formed is the moment when, because of the coming into existence of an important conjunction of external circumstances, individual group members suddenly view each other as themselves (*CDR*, I:377, 402). Suddenly, I see those who had been the Other as myself. I see each person in this particular group as a subjectivity. No longer are these persons objects. The foundation for the situation of love has appeared.

The implication in *Being and Nothingness* that, simultaneously, I must be an object that the beloved cannot transcend, and that I, in turn, must not treat the beloved as an object that I can transcend, appears in the group in fusion in two different ways: (*i*) No member of the group can transcend that group. Since my project becomes one with those of the other members, one with that of the group itself, my praxis, my project, will not transcend that of the others, for it is the same project as that of the others. Together, through the totalization of our project, we transcend our field of action towards our own ends. (*ii*) Sartre explains that each member is simultaneously transcendent and immanent. Especially at the moment that one gives some form of direction or command, that member, or third party, achieves a type of transcendence, but that transcendence is in tension with a concrete immanence in that group. Others obey the direction or command, not because the third party has been in a position of authority, but because the third party has voiced the desire of everyone. Moments later that third party participates totally in the group action. The immanence is now stronger than the transcendence (*CDR*, I:381).

----

4 The lover demands love but wants to be loved in complete freedom. Each asks that the Other not ask for anything (*BN*, 488). Also, the lover demands that the beloved remain pure subjectivity, but the moment that the beloved begins to love the lover, she becomes an objectivity swallowed up by the lover's subjectivity. Both contradictory situations lead to conflict.

Total union with the group in fusion is as impossible as Sartre showed it to be in his analysis of love in *Being and Nothingness*. He claims that this transcendence/immanence tension does not allow the members to be integrated completely into the group. At the moment of giving a direction or command, the possibility of tyranny always exists, just as, for those hearing the direction of command, the possibility of escape always exists.

But, in *Critique of Dialectical Reason*, Sartre does evolve in a more optimistic direction when he speaks of action, of praxis. That is, while implicitly continuing his stance that complete unity of subjectivities between individuals is impossible, complete unity of action is not. He states that the syntheses of third parties realize the unity of actions, not of persons. In the totalizing situation, free individual praxis objectifies itself in everyone, in the praxis of everyone (*CDR*, I:377–378). Thus, the desire of love of *Being and Nothingness*, forever thwarted, is fulfilled in *Critique of Dialectical Reason* through the medium of praxis. It is in praxis that there is no Other; the others are the same as I am. The new unity is founded upon action and, when viewed through the prism of *Being and Nothingness*, we see that the foundation of this unity, this action, is love.

This new unity lies not only within the single totalization of a group praxis, but also, within the relationships of the group's multiplicity of praxes of members with each other. It is this unity within these various praxes that forms the very stuff of history. That is, it is this unity that is at the centre of that developing action that structures the general process of praxes that produce the sweeping movement of more and more complex totalizations, the movement of history itself. The more that it is the action of the group in fusion that structures these praxes, the more the movement of history becomes the movement of love.

In *Critique of Dialectical Reason*, Sartre also speaks of the "pledge" (*CDR*, I:417-428). Just as love demands it, so too does the group in fusion, as it goes into its "statutory" phase. In the "statutory group," I freely pledge that I shall not betray the group, that I shall exist with it in a situation of fraternity. The breaking of the pledge involves terror and possible death, but the keeping of it is the foundation of my freedom. The parallel here between Sartre's concrete relations and his historical categories is quite obvious.

In *Being and Nothingness*, Sartre speaks about the degeneration of love, the result of which he labels "masochism." For Sartre, masochism is the consequence of my realizing that the unity of persons that I long for with the beloved is impossible. The subsequent despair leads me to attempt once again my goal of identity. But having failed in my original healthy project, I now attempt to achieve unity with the beloved by losing myself in him, that is, by allowing myself to be absorbed by the beloved, by ridding myself, through my own freedom, of my own subjectivity and, consequently, of my own freedom, in the midst of his subjectivity. I still seek desperately to found my being, but now, instead of seeing my subjectivity as a means to this end, I see it as an obstacle. But this act is dangerous, for with it I simultaneously deny my own transcendence. I bury myself in pure immanence, the in-itself, an action which for Sartre is a betrayal of the for-itself (what I perceive as my conscious self) whose every action should involve a transcendence of the inertia of the in-itself towards one's future. This abdication of my subjectivity, my freedom, my transcendence, the basic characteristics of the for-itself, means that I experience the beloved's surpassing me towards his own ends. In spite of my original project, my actual project now becomes to make myself into an object, an object of desire, an in-itself, a total perversion of what Sartre refers to as the "God project," the primary project of every human being: the project of becoming a for-itself-in-itself (*BN*, 476). Perhaps the most lethal part of my abdication of this primary project is that I enjoy my shame of objectivity, the giving up of my freedom, my transcendence.

In the group in fusion, the individual is absolutely essential, a situation which means that no individual in the group can ever be transcended by any other member of the group or by the group itself. But when the group becomes degraded, when the individual is constituted as inessential in relation to her function (*CDR*, I:600), that is, when the individual is considered to be less important than her function, when the function posits itself for itself and the individual is expendable, two situations are apparent: (*i*) the group in fusion is dead, and (*ii*) the institution has arrived.

What has really occurred is that the individual is no longer a member of a group which cannot transcend her, cannot use her as a means to an end. Instead, she is now a part of an institution that defines her as "the inessential means of its [own] perpetuation" (*CDR*, I:601). She has willingly given up her own subjectivity, her own transcendence and freedom to the institution so that she can avoid the isolation of seriality, that situation where the alienated individual has no real relationship with any of the categories of which history is composed. Since the excitement of the unity of the group in fusion and its subsequent sense of meaning and love are now gone, she desperately seeks the lost sense of unity in the institution. A feeling of relief, if not of real happiness, accompanies this absorption into the institution since she has escaped the obvious alienation of seriality.

We can now begin to see that Sartre's concept of masochism in inter-personal concrete relations in *Being and Nothingness* evolves into the public, social, historical sphere in *Critique of Dialectical Reason*'s category of the "institution." Masochism, of course, is the situation of the major-ity of the persons who are absorbed into the institution, not of the sover-eign persons or group who hold power at the top of the institutional hierarchy.

An essential change in the condition of the individual as she moves from the group in fusion to the institution is that the individual in the group in fusion always has power over herself, is always sovereign. Since the project of the individual is the same as that of everyone else, every-one else's project, as well as the project of the group as a whole, expresses and objectifies her own sovereignty, as directly as her own project objectifies it. But when the individual enters the institution, her sover-eignty is swept up to the top of the hierarchy. For the sake of unity, the individual sacrifices personal sovereignty. The basic structure of this powerlessness lies in the fact that the project of the institution does not objectify the individual's project, for the individual no longer has a personal project. One receives commands from above concerning what one's project must be. If one finds this project compatible with one's own desires, the situation is a happy one, but not one that expresses the freedom of the individual.

The most striking condition of the group in fusion is freedom, the abil-ity to carry out a project whose origins spring from the depths of one's own desires. This freedom/sovereignty situation then gains wonderful strength, for it is then objectified in the projects of all of the other members of the group. In fact, it is this objectification of one's sovereignty in the projects of others that is the essential structure of one's freedom. For Sartre, freedom only exists within this group in fusion (*CDR*, I:402).

In the institution this freedom no longer exists. The objectification of the projects of other persons in the institution does not reflect one's own, which in essence does not really exist, and that of the institution as a whole is certainly not an objectification of one's own project. Such a suppression of the individual's personal project is surely founded upon the fundamental concrete relation of masochism where the individual willingly submerges her freedom, subjectivity, and transcendence to the will of the beloved.

The moment that the institution emerges, everyone aims to expel free-dom from herself for the sake of declining unity (*CDR*, I:606). Clearly such willingness implies a certain eagerness, a certain joy in the partici-pation of one's loss of freedom. The person who is institutionalizing

herself is willingly allowing her subjectivity to be absorbed by the institution. She is willfully allowing herself to be absorbed into a structure of
domination. She, of course, is the dominated one.

Sartre states that, whereas in the group in fusion the members are
involved in true activity (*CDR*, I:402; or, in terms of *Being and Nothingness*, they are truly living the meaning of the for-itself, human choice
and freedom), in the institution, the institutionalized persons take on
the inertia and passivity of the institution (*CDR*, I:606). Impotence
permeates them. In terms of *Being and Nothingness*, they become part of
the in-itself of matter from which they had once separated themselves
in that first moment when they became free human beings. We see now
that the consequence of relinquishing one's subjectivity, transcendence
and freedom is that one relinquishes one's sovereignty, and, consequently,
is assimilated by inertia. Obviously, the God project is failing; to be God
one must be both the for-itself and the in-itself. To sacrifice the for-itself,
with its subjectivity, freedom and transcendence, is simply to return to
the primordial condition of undifferentiated matter.[5]

Careful reading demonstrates that Sartre's insistence upon the
growing inertia of the institution reflects back upon the "in-itself"
of *Being and Nothingness*, and, consequently, connects the notions of
"masochism," the "in-itself" and the "institution." The true horror
of what lies behind masochism can be seen more clearly in the analysis of the institution, for, through this analysis, we also can understand more clearly the powerlessness, the overwhelming passivity,
that permeates masochism.

It is also within the institution that we can see arising the public, social,
historical aspect of sadism. For Sartre, sadism is the collapse of desire.
In desire, which is itself the result of the collapse of love, I attempt to get
hold of the Other's free subjectivity through his objectivity (*BN*, 511–
512). I incarnate myself, "make myself flesh in the presence of the Other
in order to appropriate the Other's flesh" (*BN*, 506). Usually the for-
itself flees its contingency, its body, towards its possibles, but in desire,
the for-itself sees its own flesh as its possible.

When I attempt to appropriate the Other's body, I cease to be incarnated flesh, and, instead, become the for-itself, the subjectivity, "the
synthetic instrument which I am" (*BN*, 516). The Other ceases to be
incarnated flesh as consciousness, and, instead, becomes an instrument,

---

5 This is the terrifying vision that constantly haunted Roquetin in Sartre's *Nausea*,
   trans. Lloyd Alexander (New York: New Directions, 1964).

a pure object. The transcendence of the Other collapses, along with desire itself.[6]

When desire collapses and sadism begins I experience myself in the face of the Other as pure transcendence. The Other becomes the one that I appropriate, that I use for my own ends, that I transcend. Sadism emphasizes the "instrumental appropriation of the incarnated-Other" (*BN*, 518). There is an effort to incarnate thoroughly the Other by force, to bind the Other's body, to use the Other's body as a tool in order to force incarnation. Sartre points out that the sadist refuses to acknowledge his own flesh, refuses incarnation. He wishes to be a pure transcendence that appropriates the "freedom captured by flesh" (*BN*, 518) of the Other. The sadist wants his victim to submerge "freely" her freedom in her flesh (*BN*, 524). The obscene appears when the sadist forces the victim to adopt postures that strip it of its acts and reveal the inertia of its flesh (*BN*, 520). The moment that the Other is wholly flesh, she becomes the image of enslaved freedom. The sadist wants the Other to identify her freedom with her tortured flesh (*BN*, 524). The victim, once a free for-itself, capable of action, of praxis and personal projects, is now reduced to theprimordial in-itself state of the fleshy chestnut tree that haunted Sartre's anti-hero in *Nausea*.

Sartre emphasizes that the will to power is not the foundation of sadism. Sadism and the will to power are simply two responses of anxiety in the face of the Other, two responses that exist on the same plane. Nevertheless, even if a will to power is not necessary for the sadist, a structure of domination is; such a structure can be viewed within the institution.

What occurs in relation to power when the institution is born is that the sovereignty that had resided within each individual in the group in fusion is now swept up to the highest structure of the institutional hierarchy. As mentioned previously, this is the moment when impotence overtakes most of the institutionalized persons. Sartre then distinguishes this sovereignty from the type that he describes in the group in fusion by saying that the sovereignty that sweeps to the top of the institution is "authority."[7] Authority, which is the essence of the structure of domination, is power over others, whereas the power of the members of the

---

6 The impossible dream of desire is "to possess the Other's transcendence as pure transcendence and at the same time as body" (*BN*, 512).

7 Sartre uses the word "power" when he describes the pledge of the statutory group. "Power" is transformed into "authority" in the institution. In what follows we shall use the term "sovereignty" to subsume both of these concepts.

group in fusion had no element of domination. Sartre claims that it is only in the institution that we see the full emergence of authority, the full emergence of the structure of domination. This structure demands a rebirth of impotence. It is necessary for "the consecration of Power" (*CDR*, I:608).

Those in the position of authority require that those institutionalized persons that they dominate be objects, instruments, means for the ends of the institution. Authority must appropriate the subjectivity, the transcendence, the freedom of the institutionalized person. All of these persons must be stripped of the kind of praxis that was the essence of the group in fusion, the praxis of freedom and transcendence. Authority demands that inertia and necessity pervade every person in the institution. Every person must submerge "freely" her freedom in inertia. Since action or praxis among institutionalized persons is an interiorization of another will, that of the sovereign, this interiorization introduces "an induced passivity" into the action, into the person herself (*CDR*, I:615). Her own activity and freedom are stolen from her, or, in terms of the sadism described in *Being and Nothingness*, are submerged in her passivity. Her freedom is captured within in-itself-inertia. The element of sadism appears even more directly when Sartre claims that the institutionalized person's interiorization of the sovereign's will demonstrates the untranscendability without reciprocity of the sovereign (*CDR*, I:614). The sadist/sovereign is pure transcendence *vis-à-vis* his victim.

When we return to *Being and Nothingness*, we are shocked to see what primordial urge lies behind this structure of institutionalized sovereignty: the demand that the victim of the sadist become incarnated flesh so that all carnal desire can be totally and forever satisfied, a desire, needless to say, that is forever doomed. The pure flesh of *Being and Nothingness* is a personal aspect of the public, social, historical inertia of *Critique of Dialectical Reason*. What authority demands is that all institutionalized persons become incarnated flesh, while it remains the original for-itself which constantly flees its flesh, its body, its contingency, towards its own ends.

In the institution, the institutionalized persons, like the sadist's victim, choose to submerge their freedom in the flesh (*BN*, 524); that is, they finally "freely" choose to submerge their freedom in the inertia of their position. They are now "free" to concretize the project of the sovereign. The binding cords of the sadist may not be visible to the normal eye, but these institutionalized persons no longer move spontaneously (*BN*, 524); their freedom to pursue their own projects is submerged totally. They obey commands.

Kafka obviously understood the shocking truth behind the power of authority in institutions. In one of the more bizarre scenes in *The Trial*

Joseph K. enters a bank, where he discovers to his horrified amazement that two persons are being beaten, tortured, behind one of the doors. Many interpretations could perhaps apply, but surely, the link between sado-masochism and the institution is drawn here in a darkly poetic manner. The violence of the torture described by Kafka perhaps has roots in the fraternity/terror of the pledge of the group in fusion. But, in the group in fusion, fraternity is more powerful than terror; that is, fraternity, not terror, is the truly operative force and prevails until a moment in which betrayal is imminent.

As long as everyone lives the pledge, "fraternity is the real bond between ... individuals" in the group (*CDR*, I:437). But the element of terror, of violence, is present in the realization that if I or my comrade betrays the group, violence will be done to us by the group. Sartre states that the individuals of the group are able to transcend individual alienation through the common freedom that accepts the violence of the pledge, but, according to Sartre, freedom is still present, even though "The fundamental statute of the pledged group is Terror" (*CDR*, I:433). Everyone takes a "pledge of death as the inert negation of any possibility of strictly individual action" (*CDR*, I:434), that is, individual action that is not one with the group project.

What occurs when the pledged group deteriorates into the institution is that the fraternity that prevailed in the group disappears and the terror and violence sweep to the top of the institution. Although many institutions may look benign, the state has the police and the military as its two most important arms. Probably most of the torture carried out in the modern world is done through the power of various states. The violence of the sadist is present; tragically, the dark vision of Kafka has real meaning in the realm of history. The violence of the pledged group was not sadistic, for not only did fraternity prevail, but also a situation of what Sartre calls quasi-sovereignty that affected all members of the group existed. No structure of domination was present, a structure required by sadism.

The very praxis of the institution is a structure of domination over the institutionalized persons since this praxis is not one with their own, not to mention the fact that even their own praxis is not really their own project, as it was in the group in fusion. Such a structure is inherently violent, although often the only form that the violence will take is the destruction of the institutionalized person's sense of meaning in life, a meaning that is derived from executing one's own personal project. Even if everyone in the institution willingly maintains the project, the violence of "power over others" continues. Furthermore, no freedom of will sustains power from below. The authority/power is not based upon consent. Rather, the consent is an interiorization of the impossibility of resisting the power (*CDR*, I:630). Sartre actually states that the institution demands force and legitimizes it. Unifying force is the content of sovereign power, which is really the concentration of terror in the single ruling individual or ruling group (*CDR*, I:628).

Each level of the institution, even though it is not located at the top, strengthens the sovereign's power by treating those on the lower levels as objects, as instruments to be used for the ends of the sovereign. Thus, bureaucracy, the "total suppression of the human" (*CDR*, I:658), is created and we can begin to see more clearly the complex structure of sadism in the institution. It is through this structure that the sovereign can manipulate the masses of institutionalized persons, as well as large groups of serialized persons outside the actual institution. These latter persons, especially, are manipulated into thinking and acting according to the wishes of the sovereign. Sartre calls this situation "other-direction" (*CDR*, I:643). The freedom-destroying power of the sadism that turns dynamic, praxis-oriented, transcendent human beings into inert, passive objects to be manipulated for the sake of the sadist-sovereign extends far beyond the institution.

What is important to stress here is the *structure* of sadism. First, there is the structure of domination on the level of the purely inter-personal, concrete relations, and on the level of the societal, historical categories. Although Sartre, in concrete personal relations, speaks of the element of flesh and its subsequent binding under torture, it is evident that the basic formal structure of this relationship is one of domination. Experience in daily living has made quite obvious the fact that most sadomasochistic interpersonal relations do not involve the actual binding of flesh, although the more extreme ones do. But, what all these relations involve is the formal structure of domination whereby one of the persons, acting as if he were really a being who is "above" the vulnerability of the flesh (which includes, of course, death), treats the other person as if she were lesser than he, a pure material, fleshly thing that in and of itself has no real consciousness, no self-autonomy, no self-direction, no ability to transcend and, above all, no right to freedom.

When in *The Trial* Kafka's Joseph K. witnesses the torture of the flesh within the inner walls of the bank where he works, the idea that such atrocities literally take place in most institutions might strike the reader as darkly humorous. Consequently, again, what is important to remember is that each of these institutions, no matter how benign, has this structure of domination, a point which the following chapter will pursue in more detail. The power of authority exists at the top of the pyramidal structure. Those at the bottom have none, although they may agree with what the authority asks of them. Nevertheless, those who are at the top act as if they were not of the flesh, not vulnerable to the vicissitudes of life, for they have the power of "life and death" over their employees; that is, they can demote or fire any employee. The employee cannot fire the person or persons at the top of the pyramid. In institutional terms, within the structure of the institution itself, only those at the bottom of the pyramid can die, not those who rule at the top. They transcend the flesh. But in relation to the world outside the institution, those in the position of authority can face external "death" threats; that is, from the point of view of those in that outer world, those in authority have retained their flesh.

When one applies Sartre's analysis to the Church, a rather chilling revelation occurs. For example, imagining actual physical torture within the confines of downtown bank towers is rather hilarious, but the hilarity ceases when one remembers the hundreds of thousands (perhaps millions) who were actually physically tortured by the Church under the auspices of the Inquisition, and the millions, such as in the Holocaust, who (while not tortured by the Church itself) were tortured and killed without one word of protest from the Vatican. This behaviour of the Church is clearly sadistic.

But what is far more important for us today is to see that the structure of the Church, the same structure which in different times engaged in physical torture, at this very moment is sado-masochistic, for its structure is one of domination. The pope has supreme authority. Then follow the cardinals, the bishops, priests, theologians and the women religious and the laity. The structure gives the pope complete authority over everyone else, especially in the present reign of John Paul II, over theologians and women religious.

The conclusion is that this structure (having the formal structure of the institution in Sartrean terms) is one of sadism from the perspective of the top of the pyramid and one of masochism from the perspective of those at the bottom. Sado-masochism is built into the structure itself. A saint such as John XXIII may come along and momentarily infuse that structure with love, but the moment that he is gone, the sado-masochistic structure takes over again. There are few saints, and besides, to paraphrase Brecht, "Unhappy is the institution that is in need of saints."[8]

---

8 "Unhappy the land that is in need of heroes." Brecht, Bertolt, *The Life of Galileo*, trans. Desmond I. Vesey (London: Methuen, 1963), 108.

To make matters worse, one may add that the Church is the institution *par excellence*, for the Church is far more authoritarian than most modern institutions, especially in the more developed world. Imagine a modern head of a European or North American state having that office for life, a president or prime minister who could in all circumstances override the congress or the parliament, or a chief executive of a large multinational corporation whose pubic policy was that no woman could rise to the executive level because the original top executive was a man and that no woman could possibly represent him. No, one cannot imagine such authoritarianism and such open misogyny. Consequently, the structure of the Church is far more intensely sado-masochistic than are those of most of the other institutions in the developed world. Remembering that sadism and masochism are caused by the failure of love, we can now say that the sado-masochism of the Church points to a tragic failure of love, of a love that was its source and purpose.

Sartre's analysis of the psychology of the sadist perhaps sheds some light upon the terrible situation of sexual repression that exists within the Church and manifests itself in the demand for celibacy among its priests and in its attitude toward marriage, artificial birth control and abortion. The sadist, according to Sartre, has a horror of his own flesh; he flees it (*BN*, 518). He refuses incarnation, but demands pure incarnation on the part of his victim. In true sadist fashion, the male hierarchy of this institution views the persons who are at the bottom of the pyramid (women) as the pure incarnation of the flesh, as pure sex, and, consequently, seeks to repress women, to refuse them admittance to the modern world. The freedom of women is seen as being buried totally in this flesh.

This entire scene is a bizarre perversion of the real Incarnation in history, which is an event of pure love. As Jon Sobrino expresses through one of his major themes in *Christology at the Crossroads*, the Creator God takes on the flesh, the humanity of the Son, just as the Son takes on the divine essence of the Creator. Thus, the Incarnation assures Jesus' freedom. In John's words, the Word is made flesh; that is, Jesus is an incarnation into which the breath of the love of God has breathed, an incarnation that involves transcendence. In the case of the institution of the Church, the totally transcendent male hierarchy, in the position of the sadist, refuses incarnation, refuses love. Love has failed and this failure causes this hierarchy to wish, in their pure transcendence, to maintain power over the women who are perceived as objects of pure flesh, as a form of incarnation into which their word, the breath of God, has never been breathed, as objects whose freedom is forever trapped inside their flesh.

This godly hierarchy dare not love women, for they must flee their flesh, and to love the women of the Church is to incarnate themselves. Fear, disgust, forever separate the transcendent ones from the incarnated. Consequently, the Church does not represent the true event of the Incarnation; instead, it represents a perversion of it. Instead of the lover and the beloved, there is the sadist and his victim.

5

Sartrean Analysis
of the Institution

To understand in greater depth the basic sado-masochism of the structure of the Church and to understand how Jesus and his message of the Gospels ultimately developed into the structure of the present Church, it is necessary first to analyze in greater detail Sartre's concept of the "institution." This theoretical framework will then facilitate the examination of the gradual institutionalization of the Church that developed over the centuries.

The Group in Fusion and the Statutory Group

For Sartre, human history does not exist as long as human individuals remain in isolation from one another. Only when individuals form groups for the purpose of doing their work in life do humans begin to create history. The simplest group in relation to structure is the "group in fusion" (*CDR*, I:345–404). This group is remarkable, usually, for its fleeting moment in history, as well as for its radical revolutionary structure of equality. All the members of the group enjoy sovereignty and freedom.[1] No one has power over anyone else. In other words, there is no statute of power in the group. In this concrete-interpersonal relations mode of interacting, everyone sees everyone else as a subject that cannot be transcended. This relation that permeates the entire group causes everyone to see everyone else as one's own self. Not surprisingly, each person is seen by herself and by everyone else as being more important than her function. Furthermore, no one's job is more important than anyone else's since everyone's project is the same, not because someone has ordered that this situation be so, but because the vision and the means by which one accomplishes this vision through praxis are shared in common, in equality, in freedom, by all. Everyone's desires, visions and methods of carrying out this praxis are the same as everyone else's and these desires, visions and methods come from one's own consciousness, not from an external command. Such a sharing means that a translucency pervades all of the relationships. A sense of understanding and constant revelation is everywhere. Consequently, a dynamism permeates the entire group, for each person feels that she has an extremely important praxis to perform, a praxis whose source comes from within her own consciousness, in spite of, or perhaps because of, the fact that since everyone desires the same project, the project of the entire group is the same as that of each individual.

The "statutory group" (i.e., the second phase of the group in fusion; *CDR*, I:405–444) has an identical structure to the group in fusion, except for one very important difference: the "pledge." The trigger for the passing from the group in fusion to the statutory group is usually some form of external threat. The perception of this threat necessitates the taking of the pledge, a pledge that has the dual fraternity/terror structure. The terror aspect means that each person has the power of death over anyone who is a traitor. But the fraternity aspect, which, according to Sartre, is by far the most dynamically operative, assures everyone of one's loyalty. Because everyone is free and sovereign, fraternity is dominant over terror since this terror is reciprocal. Thus, an intensely strong fraternity holds terror in check. The pledge guarantees everyone's security (*CDR*, I:428).

In the statutory group, one member can momentarily transcend the group through giving a command that everyone feels is the verbal expression of one's own thoughts. But this momentary transcendence is

---

1 Sovereignty is "the absolute practical power of the dialectical organism ... its *praxis* as a developing synthesis of any given multiplicity in its practical field ... it is simply freedom itself as a project which transcends and unifies the material circumstances which gave rise to it" (*CDR* , I:578).

held in check by the fraternity/terror pledge. Furthermore, everyone else has this same capability. The transcendence and consequent dominance of the "leader" who gives a command is only temporary, and, furthermore, the fraternity aspect of the pledge remains dominant. Thus, in the statutory group, the structure of love is still operative.

The raw material for the formation of the "institution" is a group in the state of degradation, of deterioration, probably a group in fusion, a statutory group or an organization. The "organization" is a group where each person is still free, still sovereign, where each person is more important than her function, but where each person's function or project is different from that of other members. In other words, a division of labour appears. For the sake of clarity, our analysis will concentrate only on the group in fusion and the statutory group as the stuff out of which the institution arises, for contrasting these groups with the institution is the perhaps best means of highlighting the distinct characteristics of the latter.

Rise of the Institution

POWER

When the institution rises from the disintegrating state of one of these groups, massive changes take place. One of the most important changes is that a "new statute of power emerges everywhere" (*CDR*, I:604). In the group in fusion, no statute of power is present anywhere, for the statute of power is the fundamental structure of domination and no such structure can exist within a situation of true equality, of mutual reciprocity, of love.

This statute, which first appears in the statutory group in the form of the pledge, is always the power of life and death of one person over another, even when the actual power to cause death is not used, or perhaps even consciously thought. That is why all structures of domination, beginning with this most fundamental one, are ultimately dangerous and threatening to any relationship of love. The moment that power appears, love threatens to decline. In the statutory group, because the power is reciprocal, love, though threatened, still survives, for fraternity is dominant. Fraternity is very active; power is really only a potential.

The true foundation of power is the "negative and limiting determinations to which [sovereignty] is subjected" (*CDR*, I:610). Thus, the foundation of power is the negative and limiting external forces that affect the basic freedom of a person, especially the freedom of praxis and its ability to synthesize all the multiplicities within a particular practical field of action. In other words, power is a negative and limiting force in relation to a person's freedom to act, to work and subsequently to be able to change the world within that field of work according to that person's vision of how reality should be. It is this negative limitation of freedom that forms the foundation of the structure of power, the basic structure of domination, and it is this structure that kills love and enters into history with full force in the emergence of the institution.

When the institution forms, the always-held-in-check structure of power in the statutory group changes drastically, for all former reciprocal relations end. Potential power is removed from the group members in general because sovereignty becomes short-circuited; that is, the sovereignty of each individual is limited so severely that it ceases to exist.

But, in order for this process to take place, two factors must be present: (*i*) the relations among the various members must be those of "circular alterity" (*CDR*, I:601) , i.e., everywhere in the group some form of space or separation within the relations must be occurring, and (*ii*) a moment of the short-circuiting of individual sovereignty must occur. It is then that the group "does not ... have any common power with which to oppose the strength of a particular individual" (*CDR*, I:626). Consequently, all the former potential power of each individual is swept toward that place in the group where the short-circuiting occurs. But this structure of power is so different from before, since it now has a univocal rather than a reciprocal structure. Power flows in only one direction, from, let us say, the one person who now holds all of the power – the one who still enjoys sovereignty and who is subsequently often referred to as the "sovereign" – to all of the others in the institution. This univocal flow of power means that only the sovereign person has the power of life and death over everyone else, and that no one else has such power over the sovereign. Now, for the first time within Sartre's analysis of his historical categories, the true structure of domination appears. He calls this new situation one of "authority" (*CDR*, I:608).

For Sartre, history only refers to the formation of these groups and institutions within time, for it is only in these situations that individuals work together to build the earth and to create history. From this perspective, the emergence of this univocal power relation of authority marks the moment in history when love dies. The persons involved do not see this death. Nevertheless, the formal structure of the relationship of love no longer exists. No longer is there a structure of equality, of the mutual reciprocal relations between sovereign individuals.

The sovereign himself is the totally other because he has the power of life and death over me, but I have no such power over him. Whereas in the statutory group one member could momentarily transcend the group as she gave orders, now the sovereign is absolutely untranscendable at all times. Since the fraternity part of the pledge is now non-existent, the terror aspect is completely dominant. The death of fraternity is the death of love, and not surprisingly, the death of love is the birth of fully developed terror, of the structure of sadism.

MISTRUST

This structure of terror gives rise to relations of "mistrust," but in order for the institution to work at all, they are transcended insofar as "everyone abandons mistrust in favour of the untranscendable third party [i.e., the sovereign], on the understanding that he will express everyone's mistrust of everyone" (*CDR*, I:625). Thus, the unity is that of mistrust. But this structure of mistrust is deeper and far more ominous than that which lies on the purely personal level, or at the fraternity/terror pledge level, for now mistrust is incorporated into the structure of power, the power of authority. The duty to betray one's neighbour to the sovereign authority, if necessary, is a tragic reversal of the fraternity/terror pledge of the statutory group where one's duty was never to betray one's neighbour.

Once individuals become institutionalized and are no longer free individuals, they mistrust any hint of the appearance, or, more likely, the reappearance of free, direct relations, for the relations point to the incipient freedom that lies within all persons in the institution. What frightens these individuals is the realization that if such free relations begin to reappear everywhere, then the monolith of the institution will dissolve. For example, the emergence of anything resembling groups in fusion is perceived as the emergence of free relations, of freedom, and therefore, of some form of dissent. Plurality is also a sign of free relations and therefore an incipient seed of revolution.

Free, direct relations are in total contradiction with the institutionalized individuals' view of the health, and therefore of the unity, of the institution. This health/unity is viewed by them as an integration, that is, "as a petrification by which alterity will be merged into an inertia of homogeneity" (*CDR*, I:623). That is, the sovereign mediation which mediates all relations and causes separation everywhere is, in the sovereign's eyes (as well as in the eyes of the institutionalized individuals), the means by which the institution becomes the unity of a petrified homogeneity. One could say that there is a homogeneity within the earlier groups, but it is vital, dynamic and alive and, because of the relations of reciprocity, is not homogeneous in the same sense. In the group in fusion and in the statutory group, the structure of the same is present, but because everyone sees everyone else as oneself, that sameness has a different meaning from the situation where the persons see each other as other. In the institution, the homogeneity has the structure of "cloneness," of conformity, not of the dynamic oneness of the earlier groups. "The ubiquity *of the same*" (*CDR*, I:621) marks the group in fusion, whereas the sovereign who "is present in everyone as Other" (*CDR*, I:621) marks the institution.

INERTIA

Inertia permeates the institution. Inertia enters the statutory group when everyone takes the pledge never to betray everyone else. The pledge, for Sartre, is the bearer of inertia, for it comprises a certain check upon everyone, although everyone freely accepts this check. In the group in fusion, no structure of inertia is present. Now, in the institution, the pledge still exists, truncated though it is.

The "clone" factor of inertia is related to the fact that the institutional praxis, now that it is rid of the freedom of individual praxis, can produce its members "as inorganic instruments which it requires in order to develop"(*CDR*, I:599). What the institution demands is that its members "liquidate the Other in himself so as to liquidate it in the Others" (*CDR*, I:605). In other words, the relation of each member to every other (unlike the situation of the group in fusion or of the statutory group) is not that of "the same," but rather, of "the other." Nevertheless, even though the relations are truly that of "the other," the institution, whose prime value is efficiency, runs much more smoothly when one of the members liquidates this otherness in herself, not by becoming "the same," but by developing the cloneness of the institutional personality in herself. Then others will be helped to develop this reified institutional personality whose essence is to define oneself according to one's relation to the institution, for true "otherness" has the dangerous aroma of incipient freedom.

The moment that one of these institutionalized persons exercises power over some of the others who are at a lower level, that person, through dress and behaviour, exercises the will of the untranscendable sovereign. The power of this sovereign Other will be accepted by everyone since each is submerged in the stultifying inertia of reification based upon the double inertia of the pledge that now is structured only in terror and upon that of the separation of seriality or alterity.

What is absolutely required of the sovereign in order to preserve the institution is that he dissolve the members' inert-being in his historical praxis (*CDR*, I:609). Thus, in spite of the freedom of the sovereign, if his praxis is going to preserve the institution, the inertia of the reified beings over whom he has authority must lie at the core of his praxis. Consequently, no matter what the praxis is, the heaviness of inertia will always be its mark.

There are moments when this heaviness of inertia seems to lighten. This situation occurs when someone is allowed to revise or to correct the orders of the sovereign. During these moments everyone has the illusion of personal freedom and sovereignty for the relations of the former group seem to return. The old relations (based upon that of the same to the same) return, but they return as Other, because everyone becomes the bearer of the will of the other. The structure of the other remains, but the illusion helps people to continue to be content with their loss of freedom.

The praxis of the group may appear in these moments to be the personal praxis of each member, but it is really the praxis of the other, that always untranscendable Other, the sovereign and his individual will. The interiorization of this other will means that a passivity will be introduced into the heart of the praxis for any relation of reciprocity with the sovereign is impossible and only a relation of reciprocity allows for the exercise of dynamism, of vitality.

Now, not only is the self of oneself other, even to oneself, but so too is the praxis of oneself. Praxis is still performed at this level, but the will that drives it is the will of the sovereign Other, as well as his needs, desires and visions, for he is the only one who is free. One's own needs, desires and visions cease to be operative. My project is always really that of another. If for some reason (probably some situation external to the institution) my own original potentialities begin to operate, either the individual is in trouble (if no one else is behaving in the same manner), or the institution is (if many persons are behaving in this same manner).

SERIALITY

"Seriality" begins to take over in the degenerating groups when inertia emerges. In the pre-institutional world, however, seriality is the state in which persons find themselves when relations of reciprocity either are broken or never have existed. Structurally, the person is separated from others, existing in a state of alienation. Sartre's famous example of seriality is the bus queue. No one in line knows anyone else and because the line is long and everyone is either anxious to go to work or to return home from work, everyone views everyone else, not as a human being like themselves who has loves, fears, desires, dreams, etc., but rather as a possible occupant of the last seat on the bus. Everyone views everyone else as an object, rather than as a subject who, like themselves, can transcend the past toward the present and future. If one were to pursue this theme further, one could see a potentially rather nasty competition arising for the last seat, especially if someone is rudely aggressive. If all is well and everyone finds a seat, the best situation that can happen is indifference. If not, maybe even fisticuffs will occur. Obviously, no structure of love exists here.

The existence of this seriality within the institution is ironic, for the *raison d'être* of the institution is to fight against seriality within and without. That is, since its purpose is to create unity, seriality is a threat. Nevertheless, the broken bonds of mutual reciprocity cannot be blamed upon the institution, as far as seriality's origin is concerned, for institutions tend to come into existence because these bonds are disintegrating within a group. The emergence of the institution simply insures that these bonds will be completely and forever broken as long as the institution exists, for the real being and strength of the institution come to it from emptiness, separation, inertia, and seriality (*CDR*, I:603). The ubiquity of non-being appears as the "ontological statute of the community" (*CDR*, I:605).The real being of the group in fusion and the statutory group is the "sameness" of everyone, the intensely dynamic bonds of reciprocity that increase everyone's freedom of praxis and freedom in love. But these dynamic bonds are a threat to the institution, for a re-emergence of reciprocity, of the sovereignty of everyone and of freedom, would mean the end of the institution.

IMPOTENCE

Seriality is one of the conditions necessary for the birth of the power of authority, for with seriality comes "impotence" (*CDR*, I:630), and if authority is going to rule effectively, without the threat of revolt or disruption, impotence must overcome the original dynamism of the freedom of the individual. Impotence must be the basic state of all persons within an institution, with the exception of the sovereign himself or of those who have the sovereign power.

Paradoxically, it is impotence that allows the action of the institution to take place. All action on the part of the non-sovereign members of the institution results from "an interiorisation of an *other will*," and therefore introduces "an induced passivity" into it (*CDR*, I:615). For true institutional action to take place, the various members must interiorize the desires, the vision, the very will of the sovereign; they must interiorize his project so that they can carry it to fruition. In order to be active, to become involved in praxis, they must be completely passive *vis-à-vis* any inclination that they might have toward a project whose source derives from their own consciousness. It is this passiveness toward anything that resembles their own personal future, their own needs, desires and visions that comprises the impotence. The relationship between impotence and inertia is a very close one indeed.

<small>ALIENATION OF FREEDOM</small>

In this situation, personal dynamism and freedom are obviously absent. All freedom is alienated along with sovereignty in the emergence of the institution. The former freedom of the individual passes from the level of each individual action to the level of the praxis of the group. Freedom now rests with the action of the group as a whole and with the individual sovereign (*CDR*, I:599). The institution, like the group in fusion and the statutory group, has a common project, but now, instead of being the personal project in freedom and sovereignty of each member of the group, it is only the personal project in freedom and sovereignty of the sovereign elite group or person.

What occurs at the level of each individual member of the institution, at least at first, is not necessarily the covert coercion that one might expect. Because both external and internal causes are contributing to the disintegration of the former group, these individuals freely choose to become part of what they perceive to be security; they are, in fact, attracted to the institution because of its efficiency and are repelled by the idea of falling into the isolated seriality of the world outside of the group and therefore outside of history.

<small>UNITY</small>

This new unity has a very dark side when compared to that of the earlier groups. In the earlier groups, unity is based upon the actual "hereness" of everyone. Because I view everyone else as a subject (as myself, as the *same*, in a very real structural sense), everyone is "here" where I am. The unity is based upon the reciprocity of subjects, the reciprocity of love. But in the institution the structure of "here" is absent and the structure of "there" takes its place (*CDR*, I:614-615). I no longer view anyone else as subject, and, even if I still did, since reciprocal relations have been broken, the mediation of the sovereign makes them "over there," separated from myself. This separation Sartre refers to as "alterity," and it is this alterity that comprises the basic unity of the institution, not the intense structural reciprocity of the group in fusion and of the statutory group (*CDR*, I:614-615).

Now the statement that emptiness and separation are the real being of the institution comes more sharply into focus. This emptiness, separation, or distance contributes to my seeing the other members of the institution as the "other," and to my seeing the sovereign as the total or absolute Other. Contributing to this sense of otherness is the fact that the mediated distance to the other persons has become a situation of opacity, rather than translucence, as in the case of the earlier groups. Now I can no longer know directly what each member is thinking, feeling, dreaming or doing, because she is no longer me. Nor can she know anything directly about me. The relations are those of mediated opacity.

FORCE

When the institution is first formed, in spite of the fact that the individuals of the disintegrating group willingly divest themselves of their freedom in order to enjoy the security of the institution, the group is not able to oppose the individual who assumes sovereign power, for the essence of the unifying power of the authority of the sovereign is "force." Sartre claims that "force is both the right and the duty of authority" (*CDR*, I:628). The basis of this force is terror.

The sense of threat, basic to the structure of force, seems to be an essential part of the structure of sovereign authority. Sartre says, that sovereign authority "always commanding obedience *here* ... is always threatened *elsewhere*" (*CDR*, I:637). Whether for real or imagined threats, terror remains firmly in place. For this reason, although freely accepted by the non-sovereign members, ultimately, the sovereign's power is not based on consent but, rather, on "the impossibility of resisting it" (*CDR*, I:630).

Illusions and Mystifications

If one still wonders why the institutionalized persons who are not the sovereign continue to work within this institution rather than to flee to freedom, it is because the perceptions of those persons suffer from a kind of inversion. They experience the life of the sovereign as if it were their own. Seen through the prism of his life of power, they see their lives a meaningful. It is this illusion that mystifies the real situation, the fact that all of the former dynamic, vital, fully human relations that the person experienced in the group have been reified. Instead of the relations being the means of intensified life, now they are the representation of death.

I allow myself to have my freedom stolen from me, if one can speak in mythical terms, for the sake of the "demon lover."[2] In order not to alienate myself to the vast seemingly amorphous outer world filled with pure matter (i.e., the "practico-inert" or the creations of human work) and with human beings who are strangers to me, I deliberately alienate myself to the "safety" of the single concrete humanity of the sovereign or sovereign elite. I prefer this state of non-freedom to what I view as the frightening freedom of the seeming infinity of seriality in the "outer darkness." I prefer the failed, the sadistic, demon lover, to no lover at all. What freedom is given to me in exchange is the freedom of that sovereign Other whose freedom I live "as a rigid absence" (*CDR*, I:616).

Furthermore, I freely give up my freedom because this rigid absence puts me in touch with the eternal. In his purely personal, biological self, as opposed to his institutional self, the sovereign, like me, is a human being who will die. But in his institutional self, because of his place in the structure, because he must absorb and dissolve in his praxis the inertia of the other members, the position and action of the sovereign are in essence inorganic, invulnerable to death and therefore, appear to be eternal. This act of freely giving up one's freedom in order to be totally dominated by an untranscendable sovereign power is an act of masochism which creates a corresponding structure.

Conclusion

In conclusion, there are various signs that mark the presence of an institution or the moment when a praxis becomes an institution: (*i*) Function becomes more important than the individuals whose praxis fulfills this function. (*ii*) The configuration of the structure and its efficient function is essential, but the individuals who make it up are inessential. (*iii*) Any attempt to change this configuration and its essential praxis becomes

---

2 In his "Kubla Khan," Coleridge places his "demon lover" in an ambiguous situation. He apparently inhabits "a savage place" that is "holy and enchanted." Thus, holiness appears to surround him, but the word "savage," although it can be read to mean "that which is untainted by human technology," can also be read to mean "brutal." The word "enchanted" can be read to mean "full of wonder," or "that which can deprive a person of freedom." The next lines speak of this place as being "haunted by woman wailing for her demon lover!" The wailing of the woman bespeaks a lover who torments, rather than loves. This demon lover seems to promise all that is holy and enchanting (full of wonder), but if one seeks what is promised, one is cast into misery, obsession, into the hell of everlasting, unfulfilled longing. The demon lover promises love, but, instead, seizes one's freedom and enchains one forever. He is power and authority, not love. He is the Master of Domination. He is more dangerous than anyone, for he poses as the Lover.

impossible without the total disruption of this structure and praxis. Thus, change is impossible.

The sado-masochistic structure of the institution can now be understood more clearly. The individual (or, in some cases, individuals) in the position of sovereign authority is in a position of complete domination over all the other members of that institution who are perceived as quasi-objects. The sovereign alone is a subject. Other members of the institution may represent and maintain this power of the sovereignty over others and may convey seemingly unshakeable commands (because they take on the inorganic inertia of the institution), but since their praxis is really that of the absolute Other sovereign operating in themselves, those in the position of sovereign authority are still acting within a structure of dominance over everyone. The seemingly dominating freedom of these intermediary individuals is only the reflection of the freedom of the general institutional praxis onto those who are viewed by the sovereign as quasi-objects. The freedom of the individual involved in the praxis of her own project (as in a group in fusion or in a statutory group) is absent. Even though this freedom may seem to appear in the fact that the initiative for some institutional praxis comes from someone other than the sovereign, this initiative has to pass through the sovereign to be interiorized by him, before the praxis can occur. Consequently, in spite of illusions, the sovereign is untranscendable, whereas everyone else is constantly being transcended by those who are carrying out the sovereign's authority and by the sovereign himself.

Thus, on the level of Sartre's historical categories, the structure of the institution is that of intense centralization, and, on the level of Sartre's concrete interpersonal relations, it is the structure of sadism. When only one of the parties on one side of the relation is untranscendable, a structure of domination exists. Sadism is present; love is not.

No structure of love remains, for the essence of love is an equality that is expressed in relations of reciprocity. For whatever historical reasons, one can look at the disintegration of the reciprocal relations of the groups as the institution emerges and say that on the socio-historical level of history that one is witnessing the failure of love.

6

Critique of the Structure of the Present Church through Sartrean Analysis

In carrying out a Sartrean analysis of the structure of the present Roman Church we shall first examine the proceedings of Vatican Council II (1962–65)[1] and the 1983 revision of the Code of Canon Law,[2] and the actions of Pope Paul VI and Pope John Paul II concerning the status of bishops, and second, look at a few moments in the history of the Church when various aspects of this structure came into place. A brief examination of what the structure is now in relation to what it once was will help to highlight some of the Sartrean concepts of the institution and their meaning.

The Present Church

The opening of the Vatican Council II on October 11, 1962, appeared to mark the end of the Tridentine era. This time, it was theologians, not the

---

1 *Vatican Council II: The Conciliar and Post Conciliar Documents*, ed. Austin Flannery, O.P. (1988 revised ed.; Northport, NY: Costello, 1975); hereinafter cited as *"VC II."*

2 Coriden, James A., Thomas A. Green, and Donald E. Heintschel (ed.),*The Code of Canon Law: A Text and Commentary* (New York: Paulist Press, 1985).

pope, who really set the agenda. Theologians, such as Hans Küng, Karl Rahner, Yves Congar, J. Courtney Murray, Jean Danielou, and Godfrey Diekmann, were the persons behind the massive movement of reform that opened the council. Among some of the reform attitudes was a shift in relation to the problem of "truth" from "the Roman-medieval-counter-reformation-anti-modernist constellation into a modern postmodern paradigm!"[3] In support of the historical-critical method in relation to exegesis of the New Testament (and, especially, of the Gospels), truth is not an eternal, unchanging system of fixed substances, of essences, that simply needs to be taught constantly. Rather, truth is a process of discovery behind which God, over the centuries, engages with us in a process of self revelation. Furthermore, the human person is not a fixed Aristotelian-Thomistic substance but, rather, is also a process that is open to profound change and completely new understandings of meaning. Thus, truth cannot be contained in "doctrine," something that is fixed, eternal and inert. Instead, truth is an open process of communication among human beings, a process that is developed through study and dialogue. In support of this attitude, one of the decrees of the council states:

> Moreover, centers of documentation and research should be established, not only in theology but also in anthropology, psychology, sociology, methodology, for the benefit of all fields of the apostolate. (*VC II*, 797)

Also, there was a desire to limit the power of the pope by stressing the collegiality of the bishops and the pope. Furthermore, the council also tried to strengthen the power of the laity by emphasizing the concept of the "people of God" and the biblical concept of the royal priesthood of the entire Christian community:

> That is, the faithful who by Baptism are incorporated into Christ, are placed in the People of God, and in their own way share the priestly, prophetic and kingly office of Christ, and to the best of their ability carry on the mission of the whole Christian people in the Church and in the world (*VC II*, 388).

Furthermore, "the laity are made to share in the priestly, prophetical and kingly office of Christ" (*VC II*, 768) and "must cooperate in spreading and in building up the kingdom of Christ" (*VC II*, 392). Each adult

---

3 Küng, Hans, "On the State of the Catholic Church or Why a Book Like This is Necessary," in *CA*, 10-11.

exercises "the charisms given him by the Holy Spirit for the good of his brothers" (*VC II*, 796).[4]

John XXIII, who convoked the council, was the first pope in the modern world to accept that world openly. Pius XII, who preceded him, had reacted to the world in as hostile a manner as had the pope and those conservative bishops at the Council of Trent. In his encyclical, *Summi Pontificatus*, Pius stated that the world had gone astray after the Protestant Reformation, and he subsequently attacked secularism, laicist liberalism, atheistic socialism and monopoly capitalism. John, on the contrary, opened his arms and mind to the modern world, and sought dialogue with all aspects of it, including Protestants and communists.

John XXIII practiced the "primacy of service" rather than the primacy of power.[5] He preached the Gospel rather than making doctrinal speeches He did not interfere in the life of local churches, and he renounced the tools of power: condemnations, threats, excommunication, the use of the Index and inquisitorial processes. But, unfortunately, John died in 1963, two years before the end of the council, and consequently, the structure of the institution, no longer led by a charismatic reformer, reasserted itself.

Paul VI, against the wishes of the majority (led by such persons as Cardinals Suenens, Leger, and Alfrink), made last minute changes in several key documents in order to pacify the conservative minority. Concerning the Church, he emphasized papal primacy and the independence of the pope in relation to the collegiality that the majority at the council had so stressed. For example, one of the final statements from the council begins with the words: "Together with their head, the Supreme Pontiff, and never apart from him, they [the bishops] have supreme and full authority over the universal Church," but ends with the phrase, "this power cannot be exercised without the agreement of the Roman Pontiff" (*VC II*, 566). This authoritative mode continues with the following rules concerning episcopal conferences:

> Each episcopal conference will draw up its own statutes, which will be subject to the approval of the Apostolic See....
>
> Decisions of the episcopal conference, provided they have been legitimately approved by at least two thirds of the votes of the prelates who have a deliberative vote in the conference, and provided they have been confirmed by the Apostolic See, shall have the force of law. (*VC II*, 587)

---

4 In the New Testament, the Christian community is always referred to in reference to the whole, only to the whole community of "saints," "disciples," and "the elect." The term "lay person," as we know and interpret it, occurs nowhere in the New Testament.

5 Küng, Hans, *The Church* (New York: Sheed and Ward, 1967), 472.

Episcopal conferences already in existence should prepare their own statutes in accordance with the prescriptions of the sacred council; statutes already in existence shall be revised in accordance with the mind of the council and submitted to the Apostolic See for approval. (*VC II*, 609)

The core of the reality is that

The college or body of bishops has for all that no authority unless united with the Roman Pontiff, Peter's successor, as its head, whose primatial authority, let it be added, over all, whether pastors or faithful, remains in its integrity. (*VC II*, 375)

Thus, bishops only have a consultative position *vis-à-vis* the pope. Anyone who has worked within any institution knows that a consultative position gives one absolutely no power. The unspoken message in these passages is that the pope has the freedom to govern, with or without consulting the bishops, as he wishes. Thus, little has changed since Vatican I regarding the structure of the Church which is still pyramidal. Furthermore, the pope alone has the power to call synods of bishops and ecumenical councils and to decide what topics can be discussed:

There never is an ecumenical council which is not confirmed or at least recognized as such by Peter's successor. And it is the prerogative of the Roman Pontiff to convoke such councils, to preside over them and to confirm them (*VC II*, 375–376).

He also continues to have juridical power over all dioceses. He can govern absolutely alone if he wishes:

For the Roman Pontiff, by reason of his office as Vicar of Christ, namely, and as pastor of the entire Church, has full, supreme and universal power over the whole Church, a power which he can always exercise unhindered. (*VC II*, 375)

The announcement made by the Secretary General of the Council at the one hundred and twenty-third General Congregation on November 16, 1964, made absolutely clear the position of the bishops in relation to the pope. He stated that there is no equality between the head and the members of the college:

There is no such thing as the college without its head: it is *"The subject of supreme and entire power* over the whole Church." This much must be acknowledged lest the fullness of the Pope's power be jeopardized. (*VC II*, 425)

Also, the anti-Gallicanisms of Vatican I were written into the council documents with one exception. This time infallibility is given to the episcopal college, "when, together with Peter's successor, they exercise the supreme teaching office" (*VC II*, 380).

But chapter 3 of the Vatican II documents on "The Church" is so much more indebted to Vatican I than to the New Testament that Hans Küng, in his book *Infallible?*, wonders if what was happening was the domestication of the infallibility of the pope through the infallibility of the episcopate.[6] Thus, Vatican II did not correct the power given to the pope at Vatican I. The pope, if he wishes, without the consent of the episcopal college, can still claim infallibility in any question of theory or practice concerning the Church, according to "the sacred primacy of the Roman Pontiff and his infallible teaching office" (*VC II*, 370). But this infallibility extends to many areas other than to those formally declared to be infallible:

> This loyal submission of the will and intellect [of the faithful] must be given, in a special way, to the authentic teaching authority of the Roman Pontiff, even when he does not speak *ex cathedra* in such wise, indeed, that his supreme teaching authority be acknowledged with respect, and sincere assent be given to decisions made by him. (*VC II*, 379)

Cardinal Suenens of Belgium continually fought for the true collegiality principle. He claimed that there were two types of church in conflict at the council: one, the Hildebrandine, saw the Church as a superstate under the control of an absolute monarch; the other saw the Church as a group of spiritual communities, linked together in love and through an acceptance of a papal primacy. He called for an end to the Hildebrandine papacy, the papacy of absolute papal power. Bishops would elect the pope and the laity would take part in the election of bishops.

The principle of hierarchy remains firmly entrenched in the documents of Vatican II. God "bestows upon her [the Church] varied hierarchic and charismatic gifts" (*VC II*, 352). Consequently, "the apostles were careful to appoint successors in this hierarchically constituted society" (*VC II*, 371). The Vatican II documents state, "Clearly it is the *connection* of bishops *with their head* that is in question throughout and not the activity of bishops *independently* of the Pope" (*VC II*, 426). This connection is then referred to as a "hierarchical communion of all bishops with the Pope" (*VC II*, 426). Not surprisingly, after all the positive comments about the laity, this hierarchical principle was applied to them, as well as to the bishops *vis-à-vis* the pope. For example, "Like all Christians, the laity

---

6 Küng, Hans, *Infallible?*, trans. Edward Quinn (Garden City, NY: Doubleday, 1971), 80.

should promptly accept in Christian obedience what is decided by the pastors who, as teachers and rulers of the Church, represent Christ" (*VC II*, 395). Thus, even though there should be "constant dialogue with the laity [involving] painstaking search for methods capable of making apostolic action more fruitful" (*VC II*, 791), as participants in the building of the kingdom on earth, the laity obviously has only an advisory role.

On September 15, 1965, Paul VI instituted the Synod of Bishops but gave it only an advisory character. In October 1969, the Suenens group lost the struggle when the second synod of bishops agreed to allow the pope to have complete freedom in his governing role and in his teaching authority. The final document of the synod of 1980, *Familiaris Consortio*, ignored the findings of individual discussion groups and even ignored the findings of the synod as a whole. A representative of the curia so openly checked the American bishops that they got up and left in protest.

In 1968, Paul VI proved that Vatican II really changed nothing in relation to papal infallibility when he issued the famous encyclical, *Humanae Vitae*, the encyclical that declared that artificial birth control was totally unacceptable. Although this teaching is not officially infallible, in reality it is. The concepts of faith and of morals can, and easily do, creep out of their usual context into almost any area they choose. But what was most disconcerting about the encyclical was the absolutist manner in which it was carried out. Paul VI issued his stance on artificial birth control against the advice of a committee of experts whose purpose was to investigate the matter and then to advise the pope. Paul refused their expertise and advice and acted according to the absolutist structure of his position.

In 1985, Rome called an extraordinary synod of bishops. For *ordinary* synods, bishops can elect their own representatives. However, because it was an *extraordinary* synod, only the more conservative presidents of episcopal conferences and those approved by Rome had seats. The synod of bishops system, as it operates in practice, supports, rather than checks, the primacy of the pope.

It has become clear, especially under the pontificate of John Paul II, not only that the papacy is structured as an absolute monarchy, but also that the situation is getting worse. For example, Vatican II called for the establishment of priests' senates and of pastoral councils that would include laity, but John Paul II refused to have any consultation with the democratically elected Dutch National Pastoral Council when he elected two staunchly conservative men to the episcopate. The Dutch episcopate protested the entire action, but John Paul paid them no heed.

In response to this type of behaviour, in November 1987, Canadian Archbishop Donat Chiasson returned from the Synod of the Laity and stated:

> Bishops hoping for meaningful dialogue found themselves lectured to by the Vatican bureaucracy ... the synod's message to the world's Catholics is paternalistic and laced with platitudes.... Vatican civil servants obsessed with secrecy made our job impossible.[7]

On January 25, 1989, one hundred and sixty-three European theologians issued the Cologne Declaration. They stated that "the Roman curia is agressively pursuing a strategy of unilaterally filling vacant episcopal sees around the world without regard for the recommendations of the local church and without respect for their established rights."[8] They also said that "collegiality between pope and bishops is being stifled by recent Roman efforts at centralization.[9] In May 1989, sixty-three Italian and twenty-three Spanish theologians followed the Cologne Declaration with similar complaints.

Cardinal Ratzinger even openly talks about the long-term strategy of appointing bishops to replace what was considered to be an open, liberal, progressive episcopate at Vatican II with those who will follow exactly the Vatican doctrinal line.[10] For example, all must agree with Rome on "priestly celibacy, birth control, ordination of women, general absolution and annulments, etc."[11] Before appointment, new bishops are actually tested for orthodoxy and must swear to continue to follow it if they pass the test.

Many of the promises for change that Vatican II did call for have been aborted. Vatican II proposed that there be councils of laity, both in the dioceses and in the parishes. While they were to be simply advisory, they did represent a move toward greater participation in the life of the Church. But no lay councils have been established. Many changes were implemented in the liturgy, such as the use of vernacular languages and the priest's saying the Mass while facing the people, but many other changes that were in the making in various parts of the world came to

---

7 *National Catholic Register*, November 13, 1987.

8 *Origins*, Vol. 18, 1988-89, Nos. 1-36, March 2, 1989, National Catholic News Service, Washington, Thomas N. Lorsung Dir. and Ed., 633.

9 Ibid., 633.

10 Küng, Hans, "Cardinal Ratzinger, Pope Wojtyla, and Fear at the Vatican: An Open Word After a Long Silence," in *CA*, 72.

11 Schmidt, Ted, *Globe and Mail*, Toronto, August 23, 1989.

an authoritative halt in 1975. Vatican II had called for legitimate pluriformity in such areas as liturgy, theology, and organizational structure, but, now, the longing of the institution for uniformity dominates. The Roman Congregation for the Sacraments sent an order to the episcopal conference to stop all work on liturgical change. The conference had been working on an Indian liturgy. In relation to the very end of the Mass, the bishops had wished to change the command, "Go in peace" to a more egalitarian, "Let us go in peace." According to the curial order, the imperative command had to remain.

Furthermore, the ecumenical movement begun by Vatican II, which seemed to be so promising, is considered by theologians to be dead. Perhaps the greatest hopes had been held in relation to the Anglican Church. But when some sections of the Anglican Church began to admit women to the priesthood, John Paul II made clear that such an action was an obstacle to meaningful dialogue with the Roman Catholic Church. The admittance of women to the ministry on the part of many Protestant churches proved to be a similar obstacle to dialogue. It was once hoped that Protestants, Catholics and Anglicans could partake of each other's holy communion, but all opening in that direction has ceased.

Behind much of the blocking of meaningful dialogue with the Protestants is surely Cardinal Ratzinger's attitude, which he made clear in his *Ratzinger's Report on the Faith* of 1985.[12] In that document, he states that the Protestant Reformation was the beginning of modern decadence. Luther was simply an un-Catholic heretic. Furthermore, Protestantism has no validly ordained ministers or a valid Eucharist. Finally, Ratzinger rejects the Enlightenment and anything that has roots in the Reformation.

Added to this situation is the fact that John Paul II, coming from an all-Catholic country, apparently sees no need for the ecumenical movement. Having been born and raised in a country that experienced neither the Reformation nor the Enlightenment seems to have predisposed John Paul II to wish to stop both the conciliar and the ecumenical movements. The fact that he is making preparations for the beatification of Pius IX tells us much about his ideology.

The 1983 Code of Canon Law stands as testimony to the rolling back of the more positive aspects of the spirit of Vatican II, to the legitimatizing of the more regressive aspects, and to the fact that the Church has achieved an extreme degree of institutionalization. Furthermore, it sets

---

12   Ratzinger, Joseph Cardinal, *The Ratzinger Report: An Exclusive Interview on the State of the Church* (San Francisco: Ignatius Press, c. 1985).

into Church law the more regressive aspects of the council. For example, the new canon law sets virtually no limits to the power of the pope.

> The bishop of the Church of Rome, in whom resides the office given in a special way by the Lord to Peter, first of the Apostles and to be transmitted to his successors, is head of the college of bishops, the Vicar of Christ and Pastor of the universal Church on earth; therefore, in virtue of his office he enjoys supreme, full, immediate and universal ordinary power in the Church, which he can always freely exercise (Canon 331).

> The Roman Pontiff, in fulfilling the office of the supreme pastor of the Church is always united in communion with the other bishops and with the universal Church; however, he has the right, according to the needs of the Church, to determine the manner, either personal or collegial, of exercising this function . (Canon 333, §2)

Furthermore,

> It is for the Roman Pontiff alone to summon an ecumenical council, to preside over it personally or through others, to transfer, suspend or dissolve it, and to approve its decrees. (Canon 338, §1)

Thus, this code blocks conciliarism by lessening the importance of ecumenical councils and sets the seal on the fact that the bishops' councils are only advisory.[13] But even the matters on which the councils advise the pope are determined by the pope, for the content of the councils must be approved by him.

> It is for the same Roman Pontiff to determine matters to be treated in a council, and to establish the order to be followed in a council; to the questions proposed by the Roman Pontiff the fathers of a council can add other questions, to be approved by the same Roman Pontiff. (Canon 338, §2)

Canon 344 outlines in detail the absolute power of the pope over the synods of bishops.

> A synod of bishops is directly under the authority of the Roman Pontiff, whose rule it is to:

> 1. convoke a synod as often as he seems it opportune and to designate the place where its sessions are to be held;

---

13 Knut Walf asserts that "the new code talks about the competence or at least the collaborative rights of the conference of bishops in about ninety places.... [However] the competencies of conferences of bishops are frequently given an explicitly secondary importance (cf. Waft, Knut, "The New Canon Law – The Same Old System: Preconciliar Spirit in Postconciliar Formulation," in *CA*, 97).

2. ratify the election of those members who are to be elected in accord with the norm of special law and to designate and name its other members;
3. determine topics for discussion at a suitable time before the celebration of the synod in accord with the norm of special law;
4. determine the agenda;
5. preside over the synod in person or through others;
6. conclude transfer, suspend or dissolve the synod.

Thus, the mood of conciliarism of Vatican II is violated by the absolute control that the papacy has over the bishops of the Church. Such control by the pope over the bishops means that, again, in spite of the majority feeling expressed at Vatican II, the code has strengthened the power of the pope over local churches.[14]

Also, the code makes the laity dependent on the hierarchy. For example,

The Christian faithful, conscious of their own responsibility, are bound by Christian obedience to follow what the sacred pastors, as representatives of Christ, declare as teachers of the faith or determine as leaders of the Church. (Canon 212, §1)

This obedience must take place within the realm of thought as well as that of action. Canon 752 states:

A religious respect of intellect and will, even if not the assent of faith, is to be paid to the teaching which the Supreme Pontiff or the college of bishops enunciate on faith or morals when they exercise the authentic magisterium even if they do not intend to proclaim it with a definitive act; therefore the Christian faithful are to take care to avoid whatever is not in harmony with that teaching.

Canon 751 adds the threat that "obstinate doubt" about the truth of faith is a crime against religion and the unity of the Church and is punishable with excommunication. This attitude is an extension of the head-

---

14 Contrary to the spirit of the council, the new canon law in relation to the ordained *vis-à-vis* the unordained placed the concept of *potestas*, or power, in a position of dominance over the concept of *munus*, or service. When the code speaks of the "sacred Pastors," it uses the term *"potestas."* The notion of *"munus"* occurs only in the titles of Books III and IV and in the rather generally oriented formulation of Canons 204, §1 and 375, §2. In keeping with the stress on *potestas*, the new canon uses language (and the subtleties of language are the essence of Church law) that emphasizes the primacy of the pope even more than the documents of Vatican I. As evidenced in such subtleties as not giving the council a separate chapter as in the 1917 code, the new law subordinates the council to the authority of the pope much more strongly than in the 1917 law in which Canon 228 spoke of the ecumenical council as exercising "supreme jurisdiction" over the whole Church (cf. *CA*, 93, 96).

ings in the revised Code, which consistently use the ordering of "obligations and rights," whereas the 1917 Code tended to use the reverse – "rights and obligations." Obligations precede rights, and in the subtle language of Church documents, this order is significant. Furthermore, "in the interest of the common good, ecclesiastical authority has competence to regulate the exercise of rights which belong the Christian faithful" (Canon 223, §2).

Concerning the biblical notion of the royal priesthood of all believers of which Vatican II had guardedly spoken, restraints were carefully put into place. For example, since Cardinals Hume and Ratzinger argued that jurisdiction is always based on ordination, Canon 129 states that lay persons only have the ability to cooperate with the clergy when the power of jurisdiction is exercised. For example, Canon 766 states, "Lay persons can be admitted to preach in a Church or oratory if it is necessary in certain circumstances." But Canon 767, §1 immediately curtails this activity by stating, "Among the forms of preaching the homily is preeminent; it is part of the liturgy itself and is reserved to a priest or to a deacon." In other words, the important point is the fact that true lay preaching is forbidden. Canon 759 says that lay persons "in virtue of their baptism and confirmation can ... be called upon to cooperate with the bishop and presbyters in the exercise of the ministry of the word." Canon 772, §1, even places the type of preaching that is allowed to the laity under hierarchical control: "The norms issued by the diocesan bishop concerning the exercise of preaching are to be observed by all." Since the proclamation of the Gospel, which includes the homily, lies at the heart of Christian ministry, of the project of the royal priesthood, the laity are excluded from enacting the essence of the priesthood, from participating at the focal point of the praxis of building the kingdom. In relation to apostolic action, "no undertaking shall assume the name Catholic unless the consent of competent ecclesiastical authority is given" (Canon 216). The hierarchical control is a presence that pervades all aspects of the life of the laity. "Control" is a key concept that remains within an Althusserian silence, that silence within a text that often carries the core of the meaning of that text.[15]

---

15 Canon 230 does, however, say in three paragraphs that male lay persons "on a stable basis" in certain circumstances may take over ecclesiastical functions. Some sort of "emergency provision" will allow such functions. Nevertheless, the code is far more restrictive in the area of granting ecclesiastical jurisdiction upon the laity than is the code of 1917. The concept of "*missio canonica*," a concept that includes both laity and clergy in the area of ecclesiastical mission, present in the 1917 code, is absent in the 1983 code. (cf. *CA*, 100).

Not surprisingly, the fact that the hierarchy of the Church is composed solely of men is imbedded within the code in a manner that correctly can be termed "misogyny." Canon 1024 states very clearly, that "Only a baptized male validly receives sacred ordination." Thus, from conception, all women are excluded from the possibility of fully proclaiming the building of the kingdom of God within the institution of the Church. Even as children, women are prohibited from serving at Mass as altar girls.

Canon 1398 states, "A person who procures a completed abortion incurs an automatic (*latae sententiae*) excommunication." On the contrary, according to Canon 1397, a person (presumably a religious male) who murders an adult human being (a situation that more often applies to men) is not excommunicated:

> One who commits homicide, or who fraudulently or forcibly kidnaps, detains mutilates or seriously wounds a person, is to be punished, with the deprivations and prohibitions mentioned in Canon 1336 (Canon 1397)

that is:

1. a prohibition or an order concerning living in a certain place or territory;
2. deprivation of power, office, function, right, privilege, faculty, favor, title or insignia, even merely honorary;
3. a prohibition against exercising those things enumerated in n. 2 or a prohibition against exercising them in a certain place or outside a certain place: which prohibitions are never under pain of nullity;
4. a penal transfer to another office;
5. dismissed from the clerical state. (Canon 1336)

The hierarchy controls religious people, priests, and seminarians in many ways. Canon 608 states that "A religious community must live in a house legitimately constituted under the authority of the superior designated according to the norm of law." In practice, this law very strongly affects religious women who are practising their apostolate in the world. These women, many of them living with other religious in houses separate from the community, were ordered back into the "convent." A radical freedom, to live, within reason, where one wishes, and with whom one wishes, was taken away.

Aimed at particular liberation theology priests in Latin America, especially Nicaragua, and at a handful of North American priests, Canon 285, §3, states, "Clerics are forbidden to assume public offices which entail a participation in the exercise of civil power." Since the politics of these Central and North American priests are far more left wing that those of the Vatican, the political freedom, especially the freedom to fight for social justice in a public arena, was taken away. To insure that priests in the future be far less tempted toward such "free thinking," "The students are to be so formed that, imbued with love for the Church of Christ, they are devoted with a humble and filial love to the Roman Pontiff, the successor of Peter" (Canon 245, §2).[16]

Anyone who feels injured by the tool of excommunication or by any other act of the Church really has no true recourse to a form of judicial review that anyone who has lived in a relatively democratic society could recognize as being just. For example, "One who claims to have been injured by a decree for any just reason can make recourse to the hierarchic superior of the one who issued the decree" (Canon 1737). The problem is that the person at the higher level of the hierarchy is part of the same line of command as the person who offended the person who is appealing the case. In the case of excommunication, the implication is that the command comes from the highest level of the hierarchy and that, consequently, one can appeal to no one. No independent court system exists for persons who feel juridically wronged.

Some Important Moments in Church History When Structural Changes Took Place

The Early Church

The fundamental constitution of the Pauline communities was a charismatic structure; that is, each member had a "charism," or "gift," whether it be natural or given directly by the Holy Spirit, and each person exercised a particular charism within a particular praxis within the community. No one had power over anyone else concerning what charism should be exercised, e.g., that of teacher, prophet, healer, or administrator. Everyone decided what her own charism was and acted accordingly. Thus, office, that which is designated to one by someone else, did not exist. Consequently, one of the important structures of power was simply not in place.[17] At this moment no aspect of institutionalization was in existence. The charismatic structure meant that each person could

---

16 The code of 1917 does not have this regulation.

17 Leonardo Boff, *Charism and Power: Liberation Theology and the Institutional Church*, trans. John W. Diercksmeier (London: SCM Press, 1985). According to Boff, "the laying on of hands, giving rise to various orders in the Church ... is the root ... for the focus that would one day result in discrimination among the faith community to such an extent that the ordained kept all power in the Church for themselves," 45.

choose her own personal project. Sovereignty appeared to flow freely among these Christians.

It is in Jerusalem that one begins to see a structure within the Christian community that would lay the foundation for gradual institutionalization. Elders and presbyters were the leaders of the community. Acts sums up the position of elder-presbyter: "Keep guard over yourselves and over all the flock of which the Holy Spirit has given you charge, as shepherds of the church of the Lord" (Acts 20:28). It was a pastoral ministry, that is, one of looking after the spiritual welfare of the members of the community. The elders and presbyters had to lead the communities, to rule well and to labour in preaching and teaching and to preserve the teaching of Jesus and the Apostles. "Elders who give good service as leaders should be reckoned worthy of a double stipend, in particular those who work hard at preaching and teaching" (I Tim. 5:17). "Now I appeal to the elders of your community, as a fellow-elder and a witness to Christ's sufferings, and as one who has shared in the glory to be revealed: look after the flock of God whose shepherds you are ... not lording it over your charges, but setting an example to the flock" (1 Peter 5:1–3). The elders were seen as shepherds, thus, as having a guiding role and looked after the administration of monies (Acts 4:34–37). They also healed and anointed the sick (Acts 5:14–16). In Sartrean terms, the free flow of sovereignty that exists, for example, within a group in fusion, no longer exists, but, as yet, these leaders, with their accent on service, do not appear to occupy a place of total transcendence *vis-à-vis* the rest of the group. The tendency for such transcendence is there, but at this moment the strong sense of service causes the leaders to have this transcendence existing in a powerful tension with a sense of immanence within the group. The trajectory toward a totally transcendent pope of Rome is a very long one.

Another practice that the early Christians took from Judaism was *ordination*. It seems that the practices of ordination and the designation of elders appeared simultaneously in the Jerusalem community. In the Christian community, ordination involved the laying on of hands in order to legitimize publicly the fact that certain persons had been given a commission to exercise a particular ministry. In other words, a particular charism here was directly given, presumably by an apostle (an original witness) to another member. Not all ministries were involved in ordination, e.g., prophecy and healing. Ordination applied only to the founding and guiding of missionary churches.[18]

---

18 Hans Küng, *The Church* (New York: Sheed and Ward, 1967), 406.

Acts mentions that both Barnabas and Paul received the laying on of hands before they were sent out to found missionary communities (Acts 13:3). Acts makes clear that the laying on of hands existed during Luke's time and the pastoral letters give evidence of it, but Paul makes no reference to any form of ordination. Nevertheless, it is the Petrine structure of the Jerusalem community, rather than the Pauline Corinthian structure that prevailed and became the model for future communities.

The charismatic structure of the Church passed into history at that moment and, as Küng says, this situation is one in which "power has replaced Spirit."[19] Küng adds that the "bureaucratization of charisms is the necessary historical course of any religion, ... [but it is also] a narrowing, an impoverishment."[20]

The passing of Paul meant also the passing of the primacy of "*diakonia*," the concept of "service." *Diakonia* was an essential character of discipleship:

> [T]he greatest among you must bear himself like the youngest, the one who rules like one who serves. For who is the greater – the one who sits at table, or the servant who waits on him? Surely the one who sits at table. Yet I am among you like a servant. (Luke 22:26–27)

His apostleship is an office of service. "It is not that we have control of your faith; rather we are working with you for your happiness" (2 Cor. 1:24). "It is not ourselves that we proclaim; we proclaim Christ Jesus as Lord, and ourselves as your servants for Jesus' sake" (2 Cor. 4:5), and "whoever wants to be first must be the slave of all" (Mark 10:44). This conception of service is radically new. It carries with it no sense of debasement, of inferiority; instead, it carries with it a new dimension of love, and of freedom, for it is a concept that refuses power over others. For Küng, *diakonia* is rooted in charism, in the special gift that each has to give to the rest of the community and that each has received from the Holy Spirit. Charism, and, therefore, the charismatic structure of the Pauline communities, was rooted in service, the very essence of discipleship, in the Holy Spirit, the spirit of God. To move beyond this point was inevitable and necessary, but the Church moved beyond this point at its own peril. The future would see that the structure of ordination, that which surpasses the structure of *diakonia*, not only would create a priestly caste of special status, a process that would sever totally all

---

19   Ibid., 434.

20   Ibid., 423.

relations of reciprocity, but also, would set up gradually an atmosphere of impotence for all those who are not ordained.

Thus, the ordained one, the bishop or elder,[21] gradually became the person within the community who stood apart from the others, for he had been externally designated as the one with the most important charisms. This standing apart not only established him in a position of privilege *vis-à-vis* the others, but also intensified the alterity that was first introduced into the community with the act of ordination of elders and bishops. This act introduced alterity because of its external nature. One was not free simply to perform the administrative or pastoral charism of looking after the community. One had to be designated. But in the situation where the ordained person was "given" the two most important charisms, one can see more clearly the widening gap between this person and the rest of the community, or, in Sartre's terms, the growing alterity, for this person will begin to act more and more as a mediator among all the others.

It is this moment when the short-circuiting of sovereignty, of the true freedom of the individual, occurs, the moment that for Sartre marks the beginning of the institution, for it is now that reciprocal relations end. When the charisms of prophesying and teaching were not "given" through the laying on of hands, the elder or bishop was not considered to be carrying out the most important praxis in the community. Consequently, reciprocity of relations among all members flowed freely. But when the bishops or elders received these important praxes through ordination, because of this external "giving," relations of reciprocity were broken. Now that the *episkopoi* was a special position, no one was in a relation of reciprocity with him. Reciprocal relations were broken at this point. He now assumed the power that had been incipiently his because of ordination, but now was completely his because reciprocal relations were fully broken. He was the point toward which the former potential power of each individual was swept. A univocal power structure, the structure of authority, was established.

Sovereignty is short-circuited when reciprocal relations are broken because sovereignty is basically the freedom of the individual to engage in her own praxis as she wishes. Now that freedom is curtailed because of two factors: (*i*) a structure of domination exists over the praxis of the individual, and (*ii*) as far as the structure of the community is concerned,

---

21 The word *"episkopoi"* or "bishop" was used more and more as the Judeo-Christians disappeared soon after the fall of Jerusalem in A.D. 70.

that short-circuiting involves, not only the relations between each member and the bishop-elder, but also the relations among other members, for now the bishop relation mediates all relations. One's free direct relations with others are ended. But within the framework of the Christian community, another short-circuiting occurs. The direct relations that each member has had with the Holy Spirit are also short-circuited. That relation, which gave each individual the right to exercise whatever praxis one chose, has been withdrawn and has been completely usurped by the bishop-elder. The freedom of praxis is curtailed.

When the charisms were fluid and arose from the inner consciousness of the individuals, as in a group in fusion or in a statutory group, one individual could momentarily transcend the group as she gave, for example, some special insights from her prophetic or teaching praxis. But now the bishop was absolutely untranscendable at all times. Only he could transcend the group because, for the remainder of his lifetime, only he was given the most important charisms in the group. It is this situation that is the moment of the creating of the univocal structure between the bishops and the other members of the community and the moment that the structure of love dies, for relations of reciprocity must exist for love to be present within the structure. It is also at this moment that a real distinction begins between the "clergy" and the "laity."[22]

To say that at this moment the first real structure of domination appears, and simultaneously, that terror and sadism are built into the structure, sounds rather bizarre, for the change in structure appears to be so innocent. But it is important to be aware of Sartre's analysis. That is, sadism is built into the structure itself since the essence of sadism is a relation of domination. That such and such a person (or bishop, in this instance) will behave sadistically is unlikely indeed. Perhaps he will behave in a loving manner, but the point is that if he does, it is because he constantly transcends the structure. But the structure, like a sleeping jungle cat, lies in wait for two factors: (*i*) an individual with a sadistic personality, and, more importantly, (*ii*) a future event that will strengthen this structure, for the foundation is now laid.

The Beginning of Hierarchy

Moving from the world of the Pauline community to that of St. Ignatius of Antioch (end of first to the beginning of the second century) is to move from the world of *spirit* to the world of *power*. Ignatius' letters

---

22 Ibid., 410.

reveal, for the first time, a three-tiered structure: a bishop, a presbyterium (a collective word for all of the other *presbyters* or *episkopoi*) and deacons. This system is that of the monarchic episcopate.

In the fourth century, the bishops of Rome, Alexandria, Antioch and Constantinople were given the title of metropolitan bishops, and the bishop of Jerusalem was given a privileged position. The hierarchy of the Church was being strengthened as more and more power was swept toward the top of what appears to be a growing pyramid. Furthermore, now the patriarchal system was established from which the bishop of Rome would rise to primacy.

In the fifth century, Leo I (known as Leo the Great, Bishop of Rome, the first Christian to use for himself the pagan title of high priest) made an all-out attempt to bring the hierarchy of the Church to a full pyramid by proclaiming that the bishop of Rome should be the sovereign of the entire Church. But the title of "pope" was not given to the bishop of Rome until the tenth century. From the third century, the term "pope" (i.e., "father") had been given to bishops, abbots of monasteries, and later, in the East, to ordinary priests. From the fifth century, the term, "*papa urbis*" was given to the patriarchs in the East: Antioch, Alexandria, Constantinople, and Jerusalem, and the term "*papa occidentis*" was given only to the patriarch of Rome. From the eighth century, the bishops of Rome used the term "pope," rather than "*episkopos*" only for themselves. But it would be the famous Hildebrand bishop of Rome, Gregory VII, in the eleventh century, who would declare that no one else in the world deserved the name of "pope." It was at this moment that the pyramidal hierarchy, as we know it today, came more or less into place. More and more power was being swept to the very top of the pyramid, to the bishop of Rome, away from other bishops, away from the patriarchs of Jerusalem, Antioch, Alexandria and Constantinople. The schism of 1054 certainly marked the ascendency of the bishop of Rome over the bishop of Constantinople. Gaining ascendency over Alexandria was a simple task since Alexandria was under the control of the Moslems. By the thirteenth century, especially under the rule of Innocent III, the bishop of Rome clearly became the "pope" of the Christian Church of the West. The Church became the Roman Church.

In the establishment of the primacy of the bishop of Rome, all reciprocal relations within the Church were broken. Long ago, the laity (wealthy princes excluded) had lost their reciprocal relations, and, until the five patriarchates were established, the monarchical bishops (as the letters of St. Ignatius of Antioch make clear) had reciprocal relations with each other. Before that period, all bishops had shared such relations. With the establishment of the patriarchates, these five men shared such relations with one another. But now that Rome was supreme, no reciprocal relations existed within the Church. All relations were now univocal. The pope could transcend everyone, but no one could transcend him. Such absolute authority gave the pope absolute freedom, and absolute freedom means that he was in no way limited by reciprocal relations with others. At this point, all freedom within the Church, except that of the sovereign pope, was totally alienated. Structurally speaking, he alone was "subject"; everyone else was "object." The structure is one of pure sadism, and not surprisingly, the person who was in this position, as well as many who followed him into the formal Inquisition period, behaved sadistically. The best single example to site in relation to Innocent III was his ordering of the crusade against the Albigensians (Catharists) in southern France. He must take full responsibility for the massacre that followed. With Innocent III, one can see that force had become part of the institution of the Church of Rome.

With Innocent III, we see clearly Sartre's point that "force is both the right and duty of authority" (*CDR*, I:628). It is also clear that terror is the basis of this force. What perhaps is most interesting at this moment is Sartre's theory that the sense of threat (the Catharists) is essential to the structure of sovereign authority. The sovereign authority always demands obedience, and ironically this demand seems to share a gestalt existence with the feeling of being threatened. The sovereign knows that he can trust we who are "here," but what about those over "there"? Can they be trusted? Only reciprocal relations would relieve the sovereign of the unease of threat, for only within those relations does a translucence exist. Only then can one understand the desires and dreams and praxes of others. In the univocal structure, all relations are opaque, for none are direct. Even for the sovereign authority the relations are opaque because his relation flows toward others, but theirs do not really flow toward him.

Now we can see that the centralizing of power intensifies terror, for what was happening was that more and more power was in the process of being swept to the top of the pyramid. Since terror is an essential part of power, for power means some form of domination structure, more and more terror will also be swept to the top. When the reciprocal relations were first destroyed among the bishops as a whole, and then destroyed among the patriarchs, all the power that was contained in those relations moved up to the position of the sovereign. Since no reciprocal relations now existed, there was no relation within the Church that could check this power. All the power was contained within the univocal relation that flowed from the sovereign toward everyone else. Consequently, the only check upon terror was geography and lack of communication.

Finally, in 1870, at the first Vatican Council, Pius IX marked the apex of the spiritual power of the papacy when he proclaimed the infallibility of the bishop of Rome, pope of the Roman Catholic Church. Council documents[23] state that unless one accepts the fact that the apostle Peter was constituted by Christ as the prince of the apostles and as head of the Church, one will be excommunicated:

> If anyone, therefore, shall say that Blessed Peter the Apostle was not appointed the Prince of the Apostles and the visible head of the whole Church Militant, or that the same directly and immediately received from the same our Lord Jesus Christ a primacy of honor only, and not of true and proper jurisdiction; let him be anathema. (243)

Also, as the successor of Peter, the Roman pope has supreme power of jurisdiction over the Church, not only in matters concerning faith and morals, but also, in matters concerning the discipline and government of the Church.

> Peter, the Prince and chief of the Apostles ... lives, presides and judges to this day, always in his successors the Bishops of the Holy See of Rome, which was founded by Him and consecrated by His Blood. Whence whosoever succeeds to Peter in this see does by the institution of Christ Himself obtain the primacy of Peter over the whole Church. (244–245)

The subsequent canon states:

> If then, anyone shall say that it is not by the institution of Christ the Lord, or by divine right, that Blessed Peter has a perpetual line of successors in the primacy over the universal Church; or that the Roman Pontiff is not the successor of Blessed Peter in this primacy; let him be anathema. (245)

Chapter III on the power and nature of the primacy of the Roman Pontiff states:

> If then any shall say that the Roman pontiff has the office merely of inspection or direction, and not full and supreme power of jurisdiction over the universal Church, not only in things which belong to faith and morals, but also in those things which relate to the discipline and government of the Church spread throughout the world; or assert that he possesses merely the principal part, and not all the fullness of this supreme power; or that this power which he enjoys is not ordinary and immediate, both

---

23 *Dogmatic Canons and Decrees: Authorized translations of dogmatic decrees of the Council of Trent*, the decree on the Immaculate Conception, the Syllabus of Pope Pius IX , and the decrees of the Vatican Council (New York: Devin Adair, 1912).

over each and all the Churches and over each and all the pastors of the faithful; let him be anathema. (250)

The culmination of this strengthening of the power of the papacy was the statement concerning infallibility:

> We teach and define that it is a dogma divinely revealed: that the Roman Pontiff, when he speaks *ex cathedra*, that is, when, in discharge of the office of pastor and teacher of all Christians, by virtue of his supreme Apostolic authority, he defines a doctrine regarding faith or morals to be held by the universal Church, is, by the divine assistance promised to him in Blessed Peter, possessed of that infallibility with which the divine Redeemer willed, that His Church should be endowed in defining doctrine regarding faith or morals; and that, therefore, such definitions of the Roman pontiff are of themselves, and not from the consent of the Church, irreformable. (256)

From a Sartrean viewpoint, the declaration of papal infallibility is the absolutizing of authority within the Church such as had never been seen before. Even Innocent III in the thirteenth century did not claim such power within the Church. The acute centralizing of this authority in relation to "truth" is really a declaration of the fact that no one within the Church has the reciprocal relations with the Holy Spirit that the pope has. Thus, with a stroke of the pen, he proclaims that no one else within the Church has a similar relation. His relations with others in the Church become more intensely univocal than ever. The structure of the degree of domination is now much strengthened, and therefore, ironically, is even more sadistic than before since the pope is now supposedly closer to the Holy Spirit, to God, than is anyone else.

Overall Application of Sartrean Analysis to the Structure of the Present Church

POWER

In the light of the real results of Vatican II, the Code of 1983, and the attitudes and proclamations of Paul VI and (especially) John Paul II, what strikes one in looking at the structure of the present Roman Church is the statute of power. The power lies within the structure of the papacy, and that power is absolute. Since the 1983 Code, that absoluteness is even more firmly entrenched. Having become part of canon law, that absolute power has become an integral part of the practico-inert of the Church. Not only is the concept of infallibility part of the papal structure (giving it a power that is usually only associated with what is an intimate part of God), but also the total control over all the bishops has become an important aspect of that structure. Such power means that all relations between the pope and the bishops are purely univocal: all relations flow in one direction, from the pope toward all others. All the sovereignty that was once part of the bishops' office, in the long trajectory that extends back to the early Church through the ages, from the incipient "bishops" of Jerusalem, the elders, to the monarchic bishops after the time of St. Ignatius of Antioch, to the patriarchal bishop system of Jerusalem, Antioch, Alexandria, Constantinople and Rome, finally has been swept from them toward the papacy of Rome. The bishops actually have no sovereignty *vis-à-vis* themselves. Structurally they can do nothing if the papacy does not give them permission, a situation that means that they are totally impotent, regardless of what activities they may be involved in on either a local or on an international level. Relations of mutual reciprocity have ceased, and therefore, relations of equality and of love.

It is in this relation between the pope and the bishops that the true foundation of power of the papacy is laid. The bishops at Vatican II, along with many theologians, were very aware of this fact, and, for that reason, collegiality, or reciprocity of relations between the papacy and the bishops, was one of the basic themes. But because others also were aware of it, collegiality was blocked. Sartre's claim that the true foundation of power is the "negative and limiting determination to which sovereignty is subjected," is at work within the Church insofar as the results of Vatican II, through the efforts of Paul VI, John Paul II and the conservatives, and the new canon law of 1983 determine the sovereignty of the bishops in a manner which is absolutely negative. The code determines the sovereignty of the bishops in such a limited manner that the sovereignty has simply ceased to exist. The Conciliarist bishops of the fifteenth century who ran the Councils of Constance and of Basel would find such limitation of sovereignty intolerable.

It is important to examine again what Sartre means by sovereignty in the light of the relation between the papacy and the bishops. For Sartre, sovereignty means the freedom of the individual, freedom that is an intimate part of a project that organizes and transcends the objective field upon which she is acting so that that field, or part of the world, is changed (*CDR*, I:610). Thus, structurally, the freedom of the bishops, especially to act as a group, has been made null and void. Consequently, for example, when meeting as a group internationally, a moment when they should have increased freedom, the bishops have none at all. They lack the means by which they can carry out their own projects, their own way in which they could rearrange the area in which they work so as to change the world. Their freedom of praxis is limited to the point of negation since they are incapable of having full control over ecumenical councils and synods and are even are incapable of calling these gatherings.

It is this negative limitation of freedom of the bishops that lays the foundation of the structure of power of the papacy. Furthermore, it is this power of the papacy that forms the basic structure of domination within the Church. Other structures of domination exist, but this particular limitation of the bishops' freedom is the fundamental one. It is at this point that love is denied, for love cannot exist where any form of domination exists. Instead, the structure of sado-masochism thrives, for sadism is the structure of domination from the point of view of the one who dominates, and masochism is that same structure from the point of view of the one who is dominated. This ultimate negation of freedom is what Sartre refers to as the emergence of authority "in its full development" (*CDR*, I:608). Power exists in the group in fusion when one of the persons momentarily exercises it before being integrated again fully into the group, but there the power is always held in check. Now no check exists; therefore, power has been transferred into authority.

With this presence of authority, the pope becomes totally other. The pope has the power to transcend all the bishops. This constant power of transcendence completely negates his ability to be immanent within the group; subsequently, he is other.

To think in terms of the group in fusion, the situation of Jesus and the Apostles[24] and of the Pauline Corinthian community,[25] the "fraternity" part of the pledge is now absent. But when the fraternity element disappears, the terror element remains. The pope has the power to negate everything that the bishops wish to do, if he so wishes.

This structure of power, authority and domination operates just as strongly *vis-à-vis* the laity. The 1983 Canon Code's stress upon the laity's obedience to the sacred Pastors in both thought and action means that the relations between the laity and the entire priesthood, as well as the hierarchy of bishops and papacy, is like that between the bishops and the papacy, except for the fact that the domination is even more intense. The inclusion of the concept of "obedience in thought" negates freedom and sovereignty not only in praxis, but also in thought. Sovereignty is taken from the innermost recesses of the laity's being. The structure of domination here extends to the mind and soul.

The domination of praxis in relation to the laity manifests itself most concretely in the Church's rejection of the concept of the "royal priesthood"

---

24 Imboden, Roberta, *From the Cross to the Kingdom: Sartrean Dialectics and Liberation Theology* (San Francisco: Harper & Row, 1987), Chapter 3.

25 Paul did instruct the Corinthian community, but he lived with them only briefly. Much instruction, of course, occurred in letters. But the basic relations of the members of the Corinthian community resemble those of a group in fusion.

of all believers, of which Vatican II spoke. In Sartrean terms, the forbidding of lay preaching by Canon 759 places severe limitations upon the sovereignty of the laity. This limitation also means that the laity are automatically excluded from the project of the pope, of the bishops and of all the priests, the project that is most central to their lives, the preaching of the Gospel. Unlike the group in fusion or the statutory group, the members of the laity are refused any participation in the project of their group, the project that is carried out only by the ordained priesthood of the Church. Thus, they are denied the preaching of the Gospel of love. Consequently, *vis-à-vis* the central project of the Church, the laity are in a situation of total impotence. Needless to say, they are forced into a state of inertia.

One may object to this statement by saying that interpreters of the Canon Law have not negated the January 29, 1973, instruction of the Sacred Congregation for the Discipline of the Sacraments, *Immensae caritatis*. This instruction authorized the appointment of "qualified persons of either sex to serve as special ministers for a given occasion."[26] These persons are allowed to distribute communion, but pastors are reminded "of the auxiliary nature of this ministry and the preference that the law gives to the service of the ordinary ministers" (650). The line between the clergy and the laity is clearly defined. The concept of the "royal priesthood of all believers" is still rejected.

Certainly, one can still participate in the project of the Church as seen from the point of view of the hierarchy, which is to make certain that it does not succumb to the changes in the world since the thirteenth century, but if one in good conscience does so, one is still in a state of impotence, for all one is doing is internalizing and, subsequently, acting upon the project of the hierarchy. The individual lay person's personal freedom in relation to the structure of the Church simply does not exist.

But of all the persons within the Church, those who are in the most painful state of domination by the hierarchy, and in particular by the papacy, are women. The relation between women and the hierarchy is the most damaging of all the univocal relations that the papacy has with the rest of the Church. It is here that the relationship is most obviously opaque. The translucent relations of groups in fusion are long ago forgotten. The present papacy has demonstrated such an attitude of misogyny that one can only conclude that the pope has no understanding of women. This opaqueness is demonstrated in the papacy's attitude toward women in its policies on birth control, abortion and the priesthood.

---

26 *The Code of Canon Law: A Text and Commentary,* edited by James A. Coriden, Thomas J. Green, Donald E. Heintschel (New York/Mahwah: Paulist Press, 1985), 650.

On May 30, 1994, the Vatican released an apostolic letter entitled, "Ordinatio Sacerdotalis." The pope states, "In granting admission to the ministerial priesthood, the church has always acknowledged as a perennial norm her Lord's way of acting in choosing the 12 men whom he made the foundation of his church" (49). The letter ends with this precise directive: "I declare that the church has no authority whatsoever to confer priestly ordination on women and that this judgment is to be definitively held by all the church's faithful" (51).[27]

The exclusion of women from the priesthood means that from the moment of conception women are automatically, forever excluded from the fundamental project of the Church, the preaching of the Gospel of Jesus of Nazareth. Lay men are also excluded, but not by a biological determination. They are, for the most part, excluded by their own free choice. This absolute exclusion from the basic project of the Church means that the relations of women to the priesthood, the hierarchy, and especially the papacy are more obviously univocal than with any other persons in the Church and are, consequently, more obviously relations of domination. In this instance, the relationship of the powerful over the powerless is more openly one of limitation and negation.

One of the results is that women are in a more acute state of "circular alterity" than are others. They suffer more not only from a felt sense of separation from the praxis of the Church, but also from a very real structural separation.

Terror, a Consequence of Mistrust

Mistrust is apparent in the reign of John Paul II and Cardinal Ratzinger in their attitude toward the modern world. They are anti-modernists, like their Vatican I predecessors. Besides the Reformation, they reject the Enlightenment and democracy, a fruit of the French Revolution. Ratzinger's statements in his *Ratzinger's Report on the Faith* indicate that he believes that the Church functions best in what he referred to as the totalitarian countries of Eastern Europe.

This mistrust might appear to be simply an academic, philosophical curiosity if it did not have concrete implications in the actual world. Attitudes of mistrust, if not properly checked, can easily lead to actions of terror. The most striking example is in relation to women. It is here that Sartre's theory that the univocal flow of power means that the sovereign person (in this case, the pope) has the power of life and death

---

27 *Origins*, "On Ordination and Women," 24(4), June 9, 1994, National Catholic News Service, Washington, Thomas N. Lorsung, dir, and ed.

over everyone else is most apparent. It is in this relation that terror is most operative. Such a theory seems to be readily applicable to medieval monarchs and modern dictators, but this particular application to the power structure of the Church becomes apparent only when the situation of the women in the Church is examined. This situation surrounds the papacy's attitude toward birth control and abortion. If one were to take this attitude seriously, one could visualize a situation in which women were forced to return to the terrifying dangers to their health that they were forced to face in previous centuries. Modern medicine is quite capable of helping women to survive childbirth, but the human body is still essentially what it has always been. Consequently, not only would multiple births per woman remove women once more from the basic projects of life in the public modern world, but also, women's health would be greatly jeopardized. In relation to the papacy's attitude toward abortion, Sartre's concept of the univocal relation that power has over life and death is more immediate. Church policy plays the role of the executioner when one considers two factors: (*i*) denying a woman the right to choose an abortion even when her life is threatened, and (*ii*) forcing the continuation of the nightmare of the back-street abortion, which has killed thousands of women.

It is perhaps in these instances (i.e., the issues of birth control and abortion) that the present hierarchy of the Church, especially the papacy, demonstrates most clearly the sadism that is inherent in the structure. One can argue that the papacy does not wish the death of women, but neither does the classical sadist. Nevertheless, death is often the result of sadistic praxis. Furthermore, one must remember that the sadist sees himself as pure spirit, as totally transcendent, whereas his victim is seen as freedom incarnated in flesh. So too, the hierarchy, and especially the papacy, sees itself as pure transcendent freedom binding in chains the freedom of women who are viewed as freedom incarnate, as freedom living in pure flesh. Of course, such an attitude is never completely revealed in the present world, but the attitude of Heinrich Kramer's (Institoris) *Maleus Malificarum* is a silence in the text of the Vatican's pronouncement concerning women priests, artificial birth control and abortion, and, as Althusser has taught, it is these silences that are really what the text is speaking. The consequence is that terror is more acute in the relations between women and the papacy than it is in any other relations within the Church.

Relations of terror *vis-à-vis* the attitude of the "threat" have become more acute in the past few years, proving more and more the fact that the univocal structure of relations in the Church has gone through a form of intensification. First, priests were threatened with the loss of their status in the Church if they became involved in politics, and recently Cardinal O'Connor of New York has threatened any holder of public office with excommunication if that person publicly supports a woman's right to choose abortion. Earlier, we examined many forms of threats that have been aimed at theologians and women in the religious life. Also, it must not be forgotten that women who seek an abortion are threatened with excommunication. These threats, the product of a structure of terror, are the result of relations of mistrust. These threats are targeted at any form of plurality, for plurality implies dynamism and freedom, and the relations of sado-masochism insist upon the chaining of freedom and the "inertia of homogeneity" (*CDR*, I:623). That is, this relation demands that the flesh of the victims be shackled to allow as little movement as possible so as to allow the sadist to savour the helplessly chained freedom that must obey his commands.

Alterity

The univocal structure of all relations means that the sovereign relation, (i.e., the relation of everyone to the sovereign) is the relation that mediates all others. That is, no direct form of relationship exists anywhere within the structure. Alterity or separation is everywhere; a true sense of unity is lost. Perhaps some religious can still enjoy this true unity in their small groups, but there is no overall sense of dynamic unity. The lay person, especially the woman lay person, is isolated, stranded in the middle of the world's largest institution. All relations are mediated by a univocal relation of mistrust that is opaque and threatening.

Alienation of Freedom

The result of the existence of these threats is that the freedom of individual praxis, having been successfully chained, converts these individuals into "forged tool[s]" (606). Inertia is then operative within the realm of the individual's personal freedom. Consequently, the intellectual world within the Church becomes moribund and the effect upon Church members in the world of public political office is that they, as former dynamic, thinking organisms, are metamorphosed into inorganic instruments of the Church hierarchy. This inertia, the result of each member liquidating the other in herself, long ago having forfeited the possibility of the "sameness" of the group in fusion, simply develops the "cloneness" of the institutional personality so that the Church can operate as a smoothly running, efficient machine. In these circumstances, the individual, having become thoroughly reified, will define herself according to her relation to the Church's hierarchy. Any form of the stirrings of an outbreak of freedom must be checked. The result is that the sovereign, the pope, is able to "dissolve their [the members] inert being in his historical praxis" (*CDR*, I:609). In other words, when the pope acts, his action is the true representation of all Church members' action. The difference is, of course, that the pope is the only one who is really free; therefore, his praxis can never be a true reflection of the praxis of other Church members. Thus, the heaviness of inertia is all-pervading.

For Sartre, since the very meaning of freedom is totally integrated with being able to choose one's own project, the chaining of one's freedom is the curtailing of any opportunity to have any project other than that which the sovereign chooses. The laity have no part in the major project of the Church, to preach the Gospel, and therefore, have no freedom within the Church. For women, of course, as has been stated, the basic project of the Church has been eliminated since conception; therefore, their basic freedom *vis-à-vis* the Church's primary project has been annihilated since conception. The project of women is simply to be biological reproducing organisms, a project that has little to do with freedom.

Impotence and Inertia

Of course, the institution is based upon the "interiorization of an other will" (*CDR*, I:615), of the sovereign's will by the non-sovereign members. Consequently, when the Vatican insists that its members act in such a manner in public, it is simply carrying out a logical conclusion of this interiorization of the will. To insist that all dissident theologians be publicly silent is simply an extension of taking for granted that they must interiorize the will of the hierarchy and especially of the pope. To interiorize the sovereign will and to act strictly in accordance with that will is the very structure of dominance-power/submission-impotence, or sado-masochism. The dominated one is not literally in chains; she does not have to be. The will of the dominator has been interiorized. The personal needs, desires and visions of the individual have been crushed.

The worsening of impotence in the most fundamental structure of the Church, that which exists *vis-à-vis* the bishops and the papacy, is quite apparent. The "safe" test that persons must pass before they are appointed as bishops demonstrates the Vatican's desire to produce its members as "forged tools." The "safe" test liquidates the otherness in the potential appointee, the otherness that all institutions produce then strive to overcome for the sake of unity. The test liquidates the otherness in the appointee, not so that he will become a subject, another "same as I" of the group in fusion, but so that he can become a clone of the pope. The pope remains a subject, sovereign and free, but the clone appointee becomes an institutionalized object. Once the person is appointed bishop, he will be better able to liquidate the otherness of clergy and lay persons in his diocese so that the rigid, inert unity of the pyramid will remain intact for the purpose of the institution is to perpetuate its unity. Persons must be molded into the reified institutional personality.

John Paul II has also attempted to homogenize and to institutionalize further the religious women by demanding that they return to the institutional clothing that they were required to wear before Vatican II. He wishes to reimpose their former otherness. Most have not complied. But this demand is an attempt to clone these women, to make them over in his image, to take away their personalities and to give them back the institutional personalities that they were required to have before Vatican II. Such persons have no personal sovereignty or freedom, and then are incapable of forming worrisome groups in fusion.

Such inertia has become more and more a part of all Church structures. The closing down of the ecumenical, the conciliar and the liturgical movements inspired by Vatican II is evidence of the institutionalized inertia that simply will not permit change. This blocking of change was inevitable (and therefore not surprising) because of the rigid, extremely hierarchical structure of the Church. What actually was surprising was Vatican II. Vatican II was one of those rare moments when the heaviness of inertia seemed to lighten within the Church. Because John XXIII was a complete random moment *vis-à-vis* the history of the papacy, he allowed an opening to change. During this time, everyone had the illusion of personal sovereignty and freedom, that as members of the Church, now they had the opportunity, for the first time in centuries, to determine their own lives and praxes in relation to the Church. But although there was a certain amount of reality in that feeling for that moment, it very soon, before the end of the council, became an illusion, for John XXIII was dead, and all aspects of the heaviness of the inert institutional structure of the Church were intact. No one could lift this heaviness because, as always, all those who were not within the hierarchy were structurally in a state of impotence. Passivity pervaded all, for all power had gone to the top of the pyramid. No one, not even the liberal theologians and bishops, the majority at Vatican II, could do anything to prevent Paul VI from blocking many of the changes that they wanted, from blocking the spirit of the council. Some of the most brilliant, well-educated, dynamic men within the Church were completely impotent in the face of the structure of the papacy, and the situation has only worsened since. All meaningful power has been taken from the bishops. As a group, they are completely confounded by impotence.

Unity

Briefly after Vatican II, one had the feeling of a vibrant unity within the Church, for we were told and believed that the Church was the people of God, and since we could all directly relate ourselves to that concept, we momentarily felt a sense of mutual recognition, that moment in the group in fusion when we recognize the other person as ourselves. For a moment, relations with other Church members became radically lucid, and we recognized in each other a person who, like ourselves, was truly a person of God, a person who could be trusted, who loved us and whom we in turn loved. This sensibility even flowed out to those who were not Church members, persons whom we had always seen as other, but with whom now we could have dialogue. This wonderful sense of unity was based upon what we perceived to be a restructuring of the relations in the Church: relations of true collegiality between the bishops and the papacy, and relations between the papacy and the laity that we perceived to be more and more transformed into relations of reciprocity.

But now that the perception of collegiality and reciprocity have been revealed to be a misperception, a sense of emptiness, of distance, of separation pervades the Church. The "reappearance" of the univocal relations of the structures of domination have again clouded relations. "Myself" in the other has been transformed into the "other" as we, the laity (and especially we women) have realized that once again, the breath of freedom and love in the Church has been superseded by structures of domination.

Force

The Church is no longer capable of raising armies against Albigensians. Those days are of the past. But threats of excommunication and of casting priests and religious women out of their orders in such societies as the United States means that priests and nuns in their fifties and sixties who choose to unchain their freedom and perform their own projects will be cast into the jungle of the streets of American pure capitalism without careers, salaries, medical plans, pension benefits, etc. This form of threat is a form of force. Armies with weapons are no longer used. In very modern fashion, this force is manifested in the realm of economics, rather than in the realm of the military.

Illusions and Mystifications

The members of the Church who remain do so because there is nowhere else to go. Outside of the Church there appears only to be an infinity of seriality. Once again, one is reminded that we prefer the failed lover, the sadistic, demon lover, to no lover at all. Furthermore, the sovereign pope, in his institutional self, has absorbed the inertia of all members to such an extent that he appears invulnerable and eternal. Thus, one is safer if one gives up one's freedom to be dominated by this untranscendable sovereign power. The structure of the univocal relations of the Church are now strengthened, for the masochistic aspect of those relations is now firmly in place.

Conclusion

Sartre's main final points concerning the institution can easily be applied to the Church: (*i*) That function is more important than the individuals of this institution is certainly true since the overwhelming majority of individuals are a priori excluded from any real function. (*ii*) The individuals who actually perform the basic functions are also inessential. The relations of the structure are far more powerful than the individuals who make up these relations. In fact, the structure overwhelms the individual. John XXIII appeared to overwhelm the structure, but the moment that he died, the structure reasserted itself and demonstrated that the structure was still that of the Tridentine Church of the time of the Council of Trent in the sixteenth century. (*iii*) Any change of the Church's structure appears to be impossible. Vatican II began to make strong efforts to change the univocal relations between the papacy and the bishops, and between the hierarchy, the priesthood and the laity, but all attempts failed and the Code of 1983 strengthened the univocal relations. The hierarchy, and especially the papacy, have behaved as if change were far too dangerous. They were correct in that they have understood that the essential of the institution is that it must endure, but never change.

Finally, the sovereign pope remains the only subject within the Church, in spite of the fact that the illusion is perpetuated that all members are subjects. The seeming subjective freedom of intermediary persons in the structure is only the reflection of the freedom of the institutional praxis, most clearly seen in the pope, onto those who are viewed by him as quasi-objects. All praxes must pass through the sovereign and be interiorized by him before any praxis by any individual can occur.

From the perspective of Sartrean analysis, the point is that the Church behaves in the manner that it does because it is an institution, and particularly because it is more institutionalized than any other institution on earth. It is older than any other and therefore has had 2,000 years of creeping institutionalization. It is the only institution to survive the French Revolution intact. Consequently, all the characteristics that Sartre points out in relation to the institution as such belong to the institution of the Church more than to any other. The fact that John Paul II has made the Church even more absolute in its papal authority than any pope before him is simply his playing his part in the continuing evolution of the Church in its march toward an unbelievable degree of institutionalization.

One of the great differences between the institution and the group in fusion and the statutory group is that the latter groups' basic project is to change the world, while the institution's basic project is to make certain that it itself does not change. The group in fusion and the statutory group, sensing that they are not permanent, do not fear change, and, instead, open themselves to it and dynamically participate in it. The institution, intuiting its inertial permanency, does everything to create further inertia, for inertia is the essence of permanency. The irony is that the lack of inertia in the group in fusion and in the statutory group causes there to be a complete lack of the inorganic, of that which is invulnerable to death, whereas the abundant presence of inertia within the institution gives it such an inorganic quality that it appears to be immortal. Consequently, the truly dynamic and alive group in fusion and the statutory group are subject to death, but the institution, where all members who are not part of the sovereign authority are in a death-like existence, is not subject to death. But the important point is that all these structures simply act according to their nature. The group in fusion and the statutory group look and move outwardly, whereas the institution tends to turn inwardly, always making certain of its continued existence.

In conclusion, the present structure of the Church in relation to the papacy is more one of domination, of absolute spiritual power, than ever before in history, and, consequently, more a structure of sadism than ever before. The individual persons in the hierarchy are not innately sadists, but the structure is, and if, as in the case of John Paul II, one of these individuals was born and raised within a totalitarian society whose governing structures were also highly hierarchalized, where the winds of democracy never blew, then a dialectic between that person and the structure of the Church works in such a way as to make the Church more and more totalitarian, more a structure of dominance and sadism. Since Sartrean analysis reveals the sexual aspect of this structure, it is not surprising that women are its greatest victims, and the issues that seem to obsess the Pope, issues that make up the "safe" test for bishops, are basically sexual.

No structure of love remains within the institution of the Roman Church, for the structure of love is based upon reciprocal relations, upon equality. The structure of love that was once there in the early Church gradually disappeared as the structure of univocal relations were built through the establishment of the office of elders-bishops, then of the monarchic bishops in the three-tiered hierarchical structure, then of the five-patriarch system and, finally, of the supremacy of the bishop of Rome in the Western Church. Gradually, the laity became more and more excluded from this process as relations of reciprocity and love disappeared. That is why, in some ways, the laity are simply an other-directed seriality that exist outside the Church.

The Church in all ways is 2,000 years removed from the freedom, the dynamic diversity of the Pauline community of the primitive Church. All evolution since then has led step by step to an institution that has gradually destroyed that original freedom for the sake of absolute power, the polar opposite of freedom. The love that was the very structure of that original community, that was the incarnation of the message of love of the Gospels, has been replaced by a structure that is a tragic concretization of perhaps the greatest failure of love in history.

7

Deviation
and Circularity

Introduction

In the introduction, I claim that Sartre's theory in *Critique of Dialectical Reason* and *Being and Nothingness* helped to explain how the structure of the Roman Church came to be an obstacle, rather than a conduit, for the original vision of love preached in the Gospels. Because it was an *institution*, the eventual development of the Church gave it a sado-masochistic structure. But more analysis is needed before possible remedies to this state of affairs can be suggested. Why is it not possible for members of the hierarchy to transcend this structure far more often than they do? Does something actually change and distort the individuals themselves within the institution? Furthermore, does the original Gospel vision itself remain intact or is it affected too? Finally, why does the institution of the Roman Church develop as it does?

In the posthumously published second volume of his *Critique of Dialectical Reason*,[1] Sartre uses two concepts which provide the analytical tools for this chapter: "deviation" and "circularity." While Sartre himself uses these tools to examine the Soviet government under Stalin, no attempt will be made to parallel the evolution of the Church with that of the Soviet government, but Sartre's concepts are invaluable in the present analysis.

Deviation

The basic concept around which Sartre builds his analysis of what became of the Bolshevik revolution is "deviation" (*CDR*, II:111, 129). In the most simple terms, deviation is praxis losing its way to its goal and meaning. At its most elemental level, deviation is a part of all praxis which inscribes itself within a material world, a world which then sets limits to that praxis. Deviation is imposed on praxis by that material world through the "practico-inert" field that it creates (*CDR*, I:67).[2] The "practico-inert" is the result of the combination of praxis and the inert material of the world that praxis works upon and transforms. In other words, change within the field of praxis (whether it be the creation of a new tool, a bridge, or a town plan, etc.) will reflect back upon the very praxis that created it, and change it. Furthermore, since this material world, as we have always known it, is a world of poverty and scarcity, the materiality of poverty (as well as the materiality, the practico-inert, of the product that it creates) is absorbed and interiorized by the praxis. The praxis absorbs the negative as well as the positive aspects of the world in which it acts. If we refer to Sartre's *Being and Nothingness*, we shall observe an even more disturbing aspect of deviation: Pure matter, or being-in-itself, is that which can never be worked on by human praxis, that which remains forever autonomous to human praxis (*CDR* II, 309). This pure matter, which is the exterior limit (*CDR* II, 309) of all praxis, lies beyond our knowledge. Its most representative sign (i.e., death)

---

1 *Critique of Dialectical Reason*, Vol. II, trans. Quintin Hoare (London: Verso, 1991); hereinafter cited as "*CDR*, II." I shall also make frequent use of Ronald Aronson's commentary, *Sartre's Second Critique* (Chicago: University of Chicago Press, 1987); hereinafter cited as "*SC*."

2 The "practico-inert" is that part of matter, or being-in-itself, that absorbs and is transformed by human work. But Sartre emphasizes that this transformed matter then, as an external force, makes an impact upon the workers themselves, as well as upon those who subsequently live in the midst of this transformed matter, an impact that is internalized.

penetrates our every act with some form of impotence. Thus, paradoxically, because it dynamically builds the earth and all humanized life, all praxis is always penetrated by impotence, by death.

The combination of the absorption by praxis of the practico-inert (worked matter), and of the pure matter (being-in-itself) causes those who are involved in the praxis to be "other" than they were, to be occupied in attaining other objectives by other means than they had originally intended (*SC*, 176, 177). The absorption by praxis of the materiality of its products, under conditions of extreme scarcity, intensifies this process to the extent that the praxis' deviation from its original intentions is so great that those intentions themselves are deviated. These deviated intentions will now work more easily with praxis, when, in the future, it becomes apparent that the products of past praxes are imposing anti-human demands. At this level of deviation, a more intense degree of deviation obviously exists than at the more elemental level where a praxis simply is itself acted upon by its own product.

The Dialectic

For Sartre, deviation is the working of the anti-dialectic within the dialectic of praxis. The dialectic is the movement of praxis within a project in which an individual reorders a practical field in order to change that field, to change the world. The dialectic is also the interior logic of the entire project whereby the individual, in a "rigorous orientation of physico-chemical processes" exteriorizes itself and undertakes its project of "reproducing its life" (*CDR*, II:386). This aspect of the praxis is the dialectic of human reason that is at one with the dialectic of praxis. Both aspects of this dialectic are the movement of human history from our distant past in which we grappled in the most primitive manner with nature in order to survive, through time, toward a future in which, according to *Critique of Dialectical Reason*, humanity has the possibility of creating its full intelligibility, its full meaning (*CDR*, I:817–818). Thus, the dialectic, in both its subjective and its objective aspects, is the diachronic movement of history through time.

The dialectic is also "a law of creative transcendence of all means toward the end, and as dissolving within it all inert syntheses" (*CDR*, II:388). In other words, the dialectic is the transcending of need (the source of all praxis), that interiorization of scarcity which is lived as a lacuna, a gap, toward a future that holds the promise of a more fully developed humanity. This dialectic does absorb the materiality of the world with which it engages, but it is so dynamic, so powerfully driven by the free praxis of the individuals who live this praxis, that it continually transcends this absorption of materiality. But when deviation becomes overpowering, the dialectic becomes frozen; the anti-dialectic of the absorption of the inert matter of the practico-inert and of pure being-in-itself and the subsequent perversions of intentions overtakes the vitality of the praxis of the dialectic. The process element of praxis-process becomes dominant; that is, the inert matter that is absorbed in praxis begins to dominate the vital dynamic of praxis. The inertia of matter, even though it may be the inertia of the practico-inert, those human products of work that dot our earth in the form of human culture, completely immures the vitality of praxis.

Circularity

Along with the concepts of the "dialectic" and "deviation," Sartre introduces the concept of "circularity" (CDR, II:235–245). Circularity is inherent in praxis. Worked matter makes its demands on the praxis that created it (*CDR*, I:340). As a consequence of altering the world around them, the individuals who participate in praxis are in turn altered by that world, which subsequently affects their next praxis. Described in this fashion, the difference between deviation and circularity is not too apparent. The primary difference is that circularity depicts the type of movement that occurs between the individual involved in praxis and that area of the work field where she works. Deviation depicts the relationship between a particular praxis and the intention from which that praxis sprang and a later praxis and praxis-intention that are born of the original praxis.

Deviation is more of a *diachronic* movement through time, and circularity is more of a *synchronic* movement through space: person-matter, practico-inert. It is the synchronic movement of circularity that makes the diachronic movement of deviation possible. Consequently, it is only when a circularity or several circularities have occurred, and it is apparent that the original intentions for a particular project have been perverted, that one can begin to speak of deviation and that deviation and circularity are intimately linked. For example, let us say that a group of persons struggle against the social institutions of a society. This practico-inert is absorbed by those persons (circularity), who then, in a later praxis, re-exteriorize this practico-inert which, within a different context, re-conditions all the people and affects their praxes (deviation).

We can see clearly here the circularity of praxis and worked matter. The praxis of the Czarist regimes produced the worked matter of the Czarist institutions. The revolutionary praxis of Stalin, Lenin and Trotsky struggled against these institutions, absorbed and re-exteriorized them in a new way: the worked matter of old (Czarist)-new Soviet institutions. After the deaths of Lenin and Trotsky, Stalin, in a struggle to establish and stabilize socialism in the Soviet Union, absorbed in his praxis the worked matter of the revolutionary praxis, and produced Stalinist institutions. Because of the synchronic circularity movement involved in each praxis of the process, the intentions involved in the last praxis will be a deviation from those involved in the praxis of struggle against the old institutions, even though the persons may be the same, or certainly of the same group.

Original Intentions of the Bolsheviks

To speak in more concrete terms before following some of Sartre's analysis of the Bolshevik revolution and its deviation through Stalinization, one can say that the original intention of the revolution was to dissolve the Czarist regime and all its oppression and to build a society of equality where the worker would be the most important person and where that same worker would be master of her own labour. To revolt against this regime was to dissolve its worked matter, its institutions and laws, the practico-inert of past praxes. The revolution was a revolt against the domination of this practico-inert, for at the core of this domination was material scarcity, underdevelopment and inequality (*SC*, 187). To look at the early works of Marx is to see that the ultimate dream of the revolutionaries was that the entire world would share in this revolution that would create a world of abundance where the individual would be able to develop all her talents, where every individual would become an artist of life. Certainly revolutionaries such as Trotsky and Lunacharsky had such a vision. For Sartre, even Stalin shared the dream of creating a completely new society where the cultural level of workers, of everyone, would be raised significantly. What happened?

Source of Deviation

1. Workers as Practico-Inert

In order to bring this economically, politically and socially backward country into the modern world quickly (the only place where such visions could begin to be realized), oppression had to be built into the praxis of the revolutionary group. The Soviet Union had to accumulate great amounts of capital and to industrialize a country that was almost exclusively agricultural, rural and semi-feudal in its attitudes. This necessity meant that a working class had to be created through "massive demographic upheaval" and through squeezing surplus labour from the workers, if not by means of revolutionary propaganda, then through police methods (*SC*, 131).

To accomplish this action, the leadership had "to destroy those workers as free practical organisms and as common individuals, in order to be able to create man from their destruction" (*CDR*, II:150). In other words, the ruling group, the Bolshevik party, had to regard the workers as inanimate, inert matter that the party could mold according to an apriori vision. The workers were seen as a being-in-itself that would be made into a practico-inert. The workers had to be serialized, massified and hierarchized (*SC*, 124).

The isolation of the leaders from the mass of workers during this period (not only in terms of distance, but also in terms of education) "helped" in this process. But, as we saw in the section on deviation, those who engage in praxis on matter in order to transform it into the practico-inert of their vision, absorb the inertia of that matter (circularity) and are subsequently transformed by it themselves (deviation). The inertia of these workers was absorbed by the leadership. Thus, one of the first elements for the potential for deviation presents itself. This inertia will contribute to hierarchalization, "will deviate praxis at its source and be re-exteriorized as deviated praxis" (*CDR*, II:136).

2. SOCIALISM IN ONE COUNTRY

The Trotsky-Stalin conflict added to this deviated praxis. Trotsky supported the original Marxist-Leninist revolutionary vision: to unite with the Western proletariat in a permanent, universal revolution. But Stalin, who believed in "Socialism in one country" (*CDR*, II:103), won the conflict. Sartre saw this concept as an ideological monstrosity (*CDR*, II:103). The original vision had been to unify Soviet socialism and the Western proletariat; Stalin's deviation, instead, abandoned the Western proletariat, and attempted to unify what had to be kept separate: this backward country and socialism.

This deviation and contradiction, which, according to Sartre, came into being because the revolution actually was incarnated within the Soviet Union, "here," rather than somewhere within the West, and represented demands of the moment, became "the root of the institutionalization of the Russian revolution" (*CDR*, II:104). Stalin's ideological monstrosity, "Inasmuch as it was to define a propaganda, a permanent character of praxis ... could be termed an institution" (*CDR*, II:104). Thus, contrary to the original intentions of the Bolshevik leaders, because the revolution was incarnated in Russia (i.e., a poverty-stricken and isolated country), permanent revolution abroad had to be abandoned, along with the Western proletariat.

For Sartre, this "socialism in one country" is the solution of the deep contradictions that caused the revolution in the first place. The basic strains of the contradiction were: (*i*) a deeply alienated, isolated history, resulting in rampant poverty and illiteracy, and (*ii*) a profound desire for cultural emancipation. The Bolshevik party knew that it must build quickly a socialism that was materially impossible to build. This contradiction became interiorized and re-exteriorized as "hidden but constantly present oppression" (*SC*, 131). The results are a movement of both withdrawal and hope. These contradictory praxes, rooted in the fundamental contradiction, are in conflict with a basic unity within the revolution. Since individuals see this "solution" as a practical one, they accept it, for, as Sartre claims, they require a "deformed object" (*SC*, 112). Then the monstrous solution is integrated into a newly reorganized project and theory and the deviation is preserved (*SC*, 112). For Sartre, this deviation is both a practico-inert result of the revolution itself and the only means of saving the revolution.

3. Stalin Replaces Collective Leadership

That Stalin himself replaces the collective leadership after Lenin's death as the individual sovereign is an integral part of the deviation process. The revolutionaries had fought valiantly to overthrow the former individual sovereign, Czar Nicholas II, only to find that some of that practico-inert form had been interiorized and now was being re-exteriorized in new circumstances in a new way (circularity and deviation). In the process of attempting to change the old society, members of the Bolshevik ruling party, absorbed, were permeated by, the inertia of that society. Old Russia, having missed the Renaissance, the Enlightenment, and the democratic reforms that had taken place in some nineteenth-century Western European countries, was mired in the authoritarian praxis of the Middle Ages. Overwhelmed by this paralyzing practico-inert, these Bolsheviks turned to Stalin to dissolve the serialization arising from this inertia. Sartre claims that the enormous task of reconstructing Soviet society demanded that authority be invested within the biology of one person. "[T]he system as a whole demands a personal sovereign in the name of maximum integration ... at the apex of the pyramid – the living suppression of every multiplicity ... in the biological indissolubility of an individual"(*CDR*, II:208).

Why the biological unity of Stalin as opposed to that of Trotsky, for example? Since the proletarian revolution succeeded only in Russia, those who were seen as internationalist émigrés, and who had a strong internationalist orientation, were dismissed as being incapable of incarnating the Russian revolution in their biological person. Stalin, who had never left Russia, spoke only Georgian and Russian, had been a militant all his adult life, who came directly from one of the most backward and brutal areas ruled by the Czar, and who consequently epitomized the raw necessity of the revolution, was the one who was seen to incarnate the revolution most completely. As a militant known by other militants, and as an individual who had absorbed the practico-inert of his own barbarous Georgia, he was the one who could, for the purpose of the mass transformation of the Soviet Union, impose enormous demands upon the workers and peasants, who was "inflexible, without nerves and without imagination" (*SC*, 160). When workers found that the personal needs that had caused them to make the revolution, overwork and underconsumption, were now part of the requirements to build socialism, it would be Stalin who could make them accept this contradiction. Stalin was the one who could do in ten years what it had taken some societies in the West one hundred years to achieve, an inconceivable achievement that was accomplished, but with the accompaniment of brutality. Stalin, the child of barbarous old Georgia-Russia, in his rough childhood and the violence of his revolt as an adult, incarnated this moment of Russian history (*CDR*, II:216).

Sartre adds that this particular individual is not required, but certain traits are. The revolution is now individualized in the person of Stalin and his particular traits will be decisive: hardness, suspicion, dogmatism, opportunism, traits rooted in Russian history (*SC*, 160, 161). For Sartre, Stalinism is the incarnation of the lacuna that lies at the core of all praxis: scarcity, and to be more concrete, poverty. But, more important, Stalin is the incarnation of the particular lacunae that lay at the core of the Bolshevik revolution: "all the inner poverties of the practical field, from the shortage of machines to the peasants' lack of education" (*CDR*, II:226).

Consequently, the "revolutionary incarnation had chosen the singular over the universal and the national over the international" (*CDR*, II:212–213). Again, deviation from original intentions! One of the results was that the Bolsheviks had to abandon some of their original principles and, therefore, had to lean more heavily on dogmas (*SC*, 160).

4. TERROR

One of the most important types of scarcity that lay at the heart of the revolutionary praxis and then at the heart of Stalinism was, according to Sartre, the scarcity of time (*SC*, 144), for Hitler was rearming Germany, and Stalin was rightfully alarmed. Galvanizing the peasants for such an industrial undertaking in such a short time required a praxis of terror that needed consolidated power and strongly contributed to the hierarchization of the government and the subsequent sclerosis of this hierarchization (*SC*, 144), a sclerosis that entered every person within the institution of the government, and within the society as a structure of inertia. This terror became a mode of radical unification and contributed to the vigorous "pure unifying power" (*SC*, 144) that Stalin needed to industrialize quickly.

Again, we see the person of Stalin coming forward as it becomes clearer that suspicion, the necessary component of terror, was an essential part of revolutionary praxis in building the Soviet Union. A combination of encirclement by hostile nations and subsequent isolation and distrust of foreigners and intelligentsia, combined with the Soviet Union's military and industrial weakness, produced a suspicion at the core of revolutionary praxis that resonated powerfully with the suspicion that was part of the habitual conduct of Stalin as a result of his personal history (*CDR*, II:213).

Thus, Stalin served the revolution and was the revolution in all its deviations. He was its deviation. Five years before his death, the situation that spawned the deviations changed, but Stalin, sclerosed by his own all-powerful position in the hierarchy, could not. This man of solitude, of withdrawal, paralyzed by his own frozen dogmas, frozen in the praxis which had saved his revolution, could not respond to a new situation with new policies. For Soviet citizens, he became the negative element which separated him from others, from his own practical field, that is, from being able to perform meaningful praxis in the world, and from their own reality. Stalin became "ossified in himself ... a source of ignorance and unawareness" (*CDR*, II:236). For example, the Iron Curtain, required by disparity in standard of living, could have been lifted slowly, but Stalin intensified his mistrust. This mistrust of the West was an extension of his original rejection of universalism between 1924 and 1928 (*SC*, 162). What was perhaps a necessity in the 1920s became ludicrous paranoia in the late 1940s and early 1950s. The situation had once required the Soviet Union to turn in on itself, but not to the extent of this extreme cultural isolation.

Sartre's Hope

In *Critique of Dialectical Reason*, II, Sartre envisions a breakthrough in relation to this great deviation. Sartre, although he does not say so explicitly, anticipates a reversal of the Bolshevik deviation, fundamentally through one of the praxes that never really deviated, and that was the praxis of raising the Soviet people from the sloughs of illiteracy to the situation of being one of the best educated peoples in the world today. This Stalinist praxis would accumulate "transformations that [would] negate it." (*CDR*, II:163). Stalinism would self-destruct as its goals were attained. The core of the Marxist-Leninist dream of the withering away of the state and the belief in the temporary character of the extreme hardships of the period of construction still operated in this deviated praxis. The seeds of radical dissent, and, subsequently, an unfreezing of the dialectic so that the deviation could be reversed, still operated.

In *Critique of Dialectical Reason*, II, Sartre suggests that an escape can be made from the whole process of circularity. In Volume I, Sartre is pessimistic. The relationship of interiority (of the individual) and exteriority (the matter and practico-inert of the external world), "the ontological and practical foundation of the dialectic" (*CDR*, II:333), prevents praxis from transcending circularity. The circle is "a totalization perpetually reconditioned by the dispersion it totalizes.... [it] ceaselessly retotaliz(es) the multiplicities that each of its practical syntheses produces within interiority" (*CDR*, II:333). But, in Volume II, for the first time, Sartre claims that such transcendence is possible, that it is possible for human beings to gain control over the whole dialectical process.

If praxis is organized in a very full and deep manner, a time may come when it will be possible to break the circle, an event that would free individuals from the albatross of the past more than ever before. This hope is founded upon the concept that the praxis of the individual is capable of transcending the practico-inert field in which she works, even though absorption of the matter of this field still occurs. The reason for this hope is that Sartre came to believe that when praxis would reach a certain level, "commutativity" or mutual interchangeability would happen. That is, at this level of praxis, we can envision the subordination of the practical external field to praxis, just as easily as we can envision the absorption of the individual by this field.

It is at this point that Sartre speaks of "guided circularity" (*SC*, 210), where individuals are so aware of what is happening within the movement of circularity that they are able to foresee negative repercussions and to respond in a manner which is in keeping with the original intentions of the original project. The practical field of praxis which Sartre had seen so long as having (to state a bit hyperbolically) a kind of Frankenstein life of its own, now is seen more as a means between the original moment of praxis and the eventual goal of that praxis. Furthermore, Sartre actually sees positive aspects of the practico-inert, such as laws that guarantee human rights. Then, in a most surprisingly optimistic comment, Sartre claims that when the real needs of the individual are met, no trace will remain of the various syntheses of the multitudes of practico-inerts that the individual absorbed in the process of fulfilling those needs. A true liberation from circularity will occur.

But for this liberation to occur, praxis must be firmly rooted in need, that which human beings really need in order to develop fully their minds, psyches and bodies, not the manufactured needs of capitalists who tell us that we need more persons in the world to drive BMWs. A vibrant combination of this need and what Sartre views as the resilience of human beings will be a permanent basis for sustaining revolutionary desires until they are met (*SC*, 242). Deviation will still happen, but human beings will be able to limit it consciously.

Perhaps the most powerfully optimistic statement of *Critique of Dialectical Reason*, II, occurs when Sartre claims that the freezing of the dialectic is only a temporary process. Dialectical Reason has tremendous power because it operates within the dialectical praxis of history. Consequently, Dialectical Reason comprehends the projects of history, and, in placing those human projects at the centre of its thought (*SC*, 221), is capable of transcending the practico-inert that its praxis creates. It is the combination of the dialectic of reason and of praxis, working as one praxis, that bears the ever-subversive message of Marx, that one day the movement of history will be brought under the conscious and collective control of humanity. When the dialectic is unfrozen, this subversive combination will begin to operate again and the trap of circularity will be broken, for "the dialectic itself [is] the law of creative transcendence" (*CDR*, II:388). Human prixis "has a non-transcendable aim: to preserve life!" (*CDR*, II:385).

The trap of circularity in the Soviet Union certainly was transcended, but not as Sartre had envisioned. As a Marxist, Sartre had in mind the transcending of the sclerosis of authoritarianism toward a society that was democratic, dynamic, but Marxist. Instead, the Soviet Union exploded! Nothing of the vision of Marx remains.

In contemplating the future of the Roman Church in the light of *Critique of Dialectical Reason*, II, the hope exists that the trap of its circularity might be transcended. But one now realizes that the alternatives are no longer simply transcendence or entrapment in circularity and deviation. The fate of the Soviet Union has revealed another: annihilation. Unless the Roman Church radically transforms itself into the concrete form of the message of love that Jesus taught, two types of death await: absolute petrification or apocalyptic annihilation.

8

Deviation
and the Church

Original Vision

Before applying Sartre's analysis of deviation to the Church, it is necessary first to speak briefly of what the original vision of the Gospels was. What vision was at the centre of the message of Jesus? The answer is the "kingdom," a term that appears about a hundred times in the Synoptic Gospels. But having answered the question in a simple manner, now it is necessary to try to see as many dimensions as possible of this vision in order to understand the full extent of the subsequent deviation.

The eschatological aspect of the kingdom is perhaps the most obvious. The kingdom is the vision of what the ultimate condition of humankind will be. It is the vision of the ultimate society, one in which the imperfections of the present society will be left behind, one in which human beings will fulfill all their capabilities, become everything that they are able to become. The kingdom is the society in which human beings are one with the Holy Spirit, are one with God.

This direct relation with the Holy Spirit takes us into the next phase of the analysis where we see that the kingdom is a vision of very special relations among human individuals. This direct reciprocal relation of everyone with the Holy Spirit will mean that all relations among the members of the kingdom will be direct reciprocal relations. Consequently, all relations will be suffused with love, with a clarity of understanding that will make all relations translucent, filled with light. It is these relations that actually create the society of the kingdom.

Because every relation is suffused with everyone's reciprocal relation with the Holy Spirit, all relations are egalitarian. No structure of domination, of power, of authority, exists anywhere. What exists here is the group in fusion.[1]

The Sermon on the Mount expresses such radical equality, such egalitarian relations. Every line of the Sermon expresses the vision of a society in which all the structures of the present society have fallen into annihilation. Everyone who in the present is in a state of oppression will be liberated from this state. Those who hunger and thirst for justice will have their hunger satisfied and their thirst slaked. Thus, the equality that will be part of the relations of the kingdom is an integral part of the great liberation that will mark this society.

Freedom certainly will be at the centre of this liberation, freedom from oppression and the subsequent ability to develop oneself to the fullest possible extent. The vitality of the love that will be present within all relations will be the dynamic that will free individuals for the realization of the vision of the Gospels that comes to it from the Hebrew Bible, especially from the Psalms: that we are gods (Psalms 82:6). Everyone's reciprocal relation with the Holy Spirit will make everyone part of the Holy Trinity, part of the divine love that flows among the persons of the Godhead, the love that actually comprises the kingdom of God as it exists now. Such love is the dynamic of freedom.

The kingdom is surely at the centre of Jesus' vision and message, but one must remember that not all aspects of the kingdom are purely eschatological. Some aspects of that kingdom could be active in the present, if individuals would put them into practice. One of these most important aspects is the concept of the "royal priesthood of all believers." Jesus was putting into practice here an idea that Isaiah had promised

---

1 Imboden, Roberta, *From the Cross to the Kingdom: Sartrean Dialectics and Liberation Theology* (San Francisco: Harper & Row, 1987), Chapter 6. This chapter applies Sartre's concept to Jesus and his Apostles. The detailed analysis depicts the relationships in this group to be radically democratic. But, most important, all have the same project: the building of the kingdom. Not surprisingly, their relationships of reciprocity, of love, are a paradigm for the structure of relations of the kingdom.

the Jewish people, that at the time of salvation the entire nation of Israel would be a nation of priests (Isaiah 61:6). But Jesus was saying that people could be a royal priesthood now if they accepted his message, his way. That idea was radically new and implied that he was liberating his followers from all old religions and from all that those religions entailed: the elitism of priestly castes, legalisms, sacrifices. His new way was one of equality, of freedom from the law of Judaism, of freedom from sacrifice and the concepts that sacrifice entails. All his followers, as a community, could have equal access to the Holy Spirit, and all were to play an equal part in discipleship, which comprised the whole people of God. Paul wrote to the Corinthian community, "[W]hen you meet for worship, each of you contribut[es] a hymn, some instruction, a revelation, an ecstatic utterance, or its interpretation" (I Cor. 14:26).

The praxis of Jesus and his Apostles and that of the Pauline communities was certainly one in which the movement of the dialectic of praxis and of history was exceedingly alive and dynamic. They launched a revolutionary movement whose effects have been felt deeply in the Western world for 2,000 years. In the previous chapter, it was demonstrated that the institution of the present Church is far removed from that original dynamic dialectic of vision and of praxis. But how did the deviations occur? Where did the first sign of the anti-dialectic occur?

Deviation

What are the first signs of deviation from the original intentions of the message of Jesus and the Pauline communities? The establishment of the elder-presbyter system in Jerusalem is this very first source of deviation that appears. The establishment of this system, at this point, is a source of deviation, rather than the deviation itself because these elders act in a non-authoritarian manner. The book of Acts implies that disciplinary authority was forbidden (Acts 15:1–19). The spirit of the message of Jesus was still very alive; nevertheless, this structure is the first small ingredient in the eventual building of a future hierarchy. The Christians who established the Jerusalem community, in the process of accomplishing this praxis, absorbed some of the practico-inert of the world in which they were formed. They absorbed the elder-presbyter structure of Judaism. That they struggled against part of the structure is evident in that they did not establish a caste of high priests. They struggled against and successfully transcended the pointedly religious and elitist aspect of this practico-inert of the past, but they still absorbed some of it and re-exteriorized it in the form of their elder-presbyter structure. Nevertheless, in them the vision of Jesus was strong and clear, and the dialectic of the praxis of the community was dynamic, for all members were still seen as full members of the community whose mission was shared by everyone. The dialectic of their praxis, transcending a religion that for them had become hardened, made rigid, by an elitist structure, transcended the need of new freedom and hope toward a promise of a kingdom that held for them the fulfillment of this need.

But a circularity occurred. The Sartrean formula would be:

> i. *the practico-inert of the Judaic religious structure:* high priests, scribes, elders, etc.,
>
> ii. *the praxis:* struggle of Judao Christians against these institutions, and a subsequent absorption and re-exteriorization of them in a new way, and
>
> iii. *the practico-inert result:* the elder-presbyter Judeo-Christian Jerusalem structure.

These Jerusalem Christians, in creating a new praxis within their environment, acted upon that environment, and in creating something new, absorbed part of what they changed. This circularity, this synchronic movement between these Christians and their Jerusalem environs, is the relation that set in motion the first source of deviation from the original intentions of Jesus toward the goal of attaining the kingdom.

The other source of deviation of the early Christian Jerusalem community occurred simultaneously with the establishment of elders-presbyters: ordination. As with the establishment of the elder-presbyter structure, we must again be reassured by Acts that the dialectic of the vision and praxis of Jesus and the Apostles was intact. Nevertheless, a structure of power, such as that of the elder-presbyters, was now in place, a structure that would lead to great deviation in the future.

What happened at this point was that inertia entered the praxis of the Church; from now on all praxis would become praxis-process because the first structure of domination was established: the elder-presbyter structure in Jerusalem. That inertia was increased with the practice of ordination. This inertia was going to be at the very source of the deviation that would gradually become more and more acute as it moved forward across the centuries – an inertia that would ultimately sclerose the Church that was once such a dynamic community.

It would appear that these early Christians, including the Greco-pagano-Christians who began using the *episkopoi*-deacon structure, had to develop these structures of power, elemental though they were, in order to preserve the message of Jesus as they saw it. Otherwise, the Church might have fragmented into such diversity that the original vision would simply have disappeared. A unity of the original vision had to be preserved. The process of ordination would make more certain that this vision was retained. The community would feel more secure in its mission if it explicitly designated certain persons to lead the community, albeit in a non-authoritarian manner, in order to make certain that this vision would remain intact.[2]

Thus, oppression had to be built into the praxis of this revolutionary group, even though, in this instance, it was a rather incipient oppression that would manifest itself in the future. Nevertheless, once such structures are in place, they simply must wait for future members to strengthen their oppressive force. These persons, unlike those who developed the *episkopoi*-deacon structure, will have had their intentions deviated by those very structures.

What occurred with the creation of the first source of deviation for the Christians was the movement of the dialectic between praxis and the practico-inert of the religious world of Judaism with which it interacted in order to rearrange the practical world in a new manner. For the Greco-Christians (who, by the end of the second century, no longer had the Pauline community structure), the source of their first deviation lay in scarcity, the scarcity of the most important persons within the Pauline community – the prophets and teachers. Here the materiality of scarcity was absorbed, interiorized by a praxis which then re-exteriorized this scarcity in a new form of the practico-inert, the first structure of domination in the Greco-Christian community: the *episkopoi*-deacon structure.

However, the moment when these structures of domination and of ordination were finalized in the entire Christian community marked the beginning of the institution. From this moment, the praxes that built upon these structures would be performed by persons whose intentions deviated from those of Jesus, the Apostles and the Pauline communities. This time, the praxis would be working upon a practico-inert of domination that would be seen as "Christian" and therefore, good. No one would be on guard to struggle against any aspects of it. No one would struggle against part of it as the first Jerusalem Christians did against the religious structures of Judaism created by the elder-presbyter structure. Thus, the basic problem is that no struggle against any

---

2 Thomas O'Dea (*Sociology of Religion*, Englewood Cliffs, NJ: Prentice-Hall, 1966, 37) states that pure charisma exists only when a religious movement is in the originating process . If we follow E. Kasemann (in Hans Küng, *Structures of the Church*, trans. Salvator Attanasio, New York: Thomas Nelson and Son, 1964, 154) concerning Gnostic radical sectarianism, and Charles Davis (*A Question of Conscience*, London: Hodden and Stoughton, 1965, 138) concerning Apostolic identity and continuity, praxis that brought inertia and, with it, the first source of deviation, proved to be a necessity.

aspect of this structure would occur and, consequently, the inertia of that structure would enter into the praxis of these Christians, unimpeded. Since the very essence of the original vision is the pure dynamism of the dialectic of freedom, of love, of the will to create a kingdom where even the everlasting hills will be transformed, any entrance of inertia into the praxis of the Christians means that deviation from the original vision has taken place within the praxis and within the intentions that were incorporated within it, for Sartre sees reason-intentions and praxis as being inseparable.

The moment that marked an even deeper penetration of inertia within praxis so that the deviation of intentions became more acute occurred with the establishment of the monarchic bishop system and the subsequent three-tiered structure that also included the presbyterium and the deacons, the first hierarchy within the Church. The amount of inertia within praxis increased dangerously because of the increased inertia within the practico-inert of the structure. From now on, the deviated intentions of Christians would work rather easily with future praxes that would operate with this new hierarchy when it imposed anti-human demands.

The anti-human demands that this hierarchy would make, of course, would be to strengthen itself, but the fulfillment of such demands, still going on at the present, would take time. The first stage was the creation of the patriarchate system. The second, was the creation of the primacy of the Roman bishop. That the bishop of Rome would eventually replace the collective leadership of the bishops was an extremely important part of the deviation process. From this moment, the process element would begin to be a powerful force in the praxis-process movement.

What occurred in the gradual establishment of the Roman bishop as the supreme head of the Church was a gradual absorption of the practico-inert of the Roman Empire and its imperial trappings into the praxis of the Church. Just as Jesus had struggled against the Judaic establishment in Jerusalem, Christians in the first centuries struggled in the period of persecutions against the Roman imperial establishment. But when Emperor Constantine became a Christian, Christians no longer had to struggle against imperial Rome. Now they could see it as "good," and the practico-inert of its imperial structure and of Roman law would begin to enter its praxis. The absorption of Roman law would make the Roman patriarchate fundamentally different from the others, especially that of Constantinople, and would make Rome more capable of strengthening itself *vis-à-vis* the others. This absorption created a circularity between the Roman Empire and the praxis of the Church that in turn created another stage of a profound deviation that would take the Church very far from the original vision of Jesus. The Church would create a powerful structure in Rome that would have far more power than the other patriarchates to make anti-human demands. The inertia that would enter with the establishment of the primacy of the bishop of Rome would begin the movement to an unending structural and spiritual sclerosis of the Church.

The statement that the structure of the primacy of the Roman patriarchate would make anti-human demands is based upon the supposition that any structure of domination is fundamentally anti-human. This supposition, in turn, is based, in this instance, upon the vision of Jesus, whose Sermon on the Mount makes clear what he thinks of structures of domination. In the kingdom, there shall be none, and the kingdom is the society of the future in which humanity shall be so fulfilled that all aspects of the anti-human shall no longer exist.

The obligatory withdrawal of the clergy from the world in the fourth century marked the first crucial deviation from the original vision that all members of the Church were members of the royal priesthood. The source of the deviation lay in the inertia of ordination, but as long as the ordained lived the lives of the unordained, real deviation was only present in potential form. The obligatory withdrawal was a praxis that worked upon the practico-inert of ordination and, in thinking that it was "good," did not in any way struggle against it. Instead, the praxis totally absorbed the practico-inert, and the result of this circularity was a praxis that was a deviation that carried with it the deviation of intention that would ultimately lead to obligatory celibacy.

With the exception of wealthy and powerful secular princes, the obligatory movement of clergy from the world began a movement that would, as far as the Church is concerned, serialize, massify the laity, and change them into the practico-inert. But was this movement necessary? It would seem that such treatment of the laity had no historical benefits. It could be argued that the gap that eventually existed between the level of education of the clergy and that of the laity made this treatment understandable and inevitable. But the difference in education still does not make such oppression an historical necessity for the sake of future generations. Nevertheless, the inertia caused by this oppression that was absorbed by the leaders in the serialization of the laity would contribute to further hierarchalization and would contribute to deviating praxis at its source.

Necessity of Deviation

One can argue that the gradual strengthening of the hierarchy until it reached its apogee of both secular and spiritual power in the thirteenth century was necessary. This radical deviation was necessary in order that the Christian message could be conveyed through the centuries, even though this message seems to have lived, as far as the structure of the Church is concerned, mainly on the pages of Scripture, as well as in the hearts and minds of various Christians, among whom one could perhaps mention such groups as the Franciscans and various monks in monasteries. Since the Church was the most stable institution to exist in Europe during much of the Middle Ages, one can argue that European civilization needed the institution whose monks toiled away in monasteries preserving what they could of human civilization as they knew it. Without such centralization, European civilization would probably have been, and would now be, much diminished. If the structure of the early Pauline communities had been the only form of Christian community to have survived the early period, it is easy to imagine that the Germanic tribes would simply have annihilated the Christian message. It is especially easy to imagine pagan Frankish kings and knights turning the visions of the Gospels into the dust of history.

Nevertheless, the Church had become, in a gigantic circular movement that was one of the greatest deviations in history, exactly what it had struggled against in its early years: a traditional religion and a structure with an imperial hierarchy. Jesus and the early Christians had eschewed the priestly caste of Judaism and had struggled, as is evidenced by Paul's letters, against the religious sacrifices of the pagans. The early Christians, including Paul, suffered greatly at the hands of the Roman Empire. But now, through a circularity that became a gross deviation of praxis and of intentions, the Church had become the mirror of that which it had seen as its opposite. The equality, freedom and love of the Sermon on the Mount had disappeared from the structure of the Church.

What occurred in this gigantic circularity-deviation was that the Church structure became a very rigidly hierarchalized, brutal structure that allowed no change. Albigensians learned this terrible truth. But, again, one can argue that this structure of the Church was necessary. We of the modern world would have preferred a less brutal structure, but the world that surrounded the Church was brutal. Furthermore, Christians lived a deep contradiction: from the beginning they lived in a hierarchalized world where structures of equality were unknown, but they dreamed of a society where they flourished. In that sense, the lacuna at the source of their praxis was a need, the need of a society where those who longed for justice would be satisfied. They dreamed of the kingdom. They absorbed this contradiction; it became interiorized and then re-exteriorized in its deviations.

The Necessity of Strong, Brutalized Popes

In the Church's various historical moments when it has been going either through particular periods of especially strong centralization or through periods of crisis, individuals of certain traits always have appeared as popes. Particular individuals have not been required, but certain traits have been: dogmatism, an authoritarian personality, and a certain degree of suspicion. Leo the Great, Gregory VII, the Hildebrand pope, Innocent III, Pius IX and John Paul II have been those who have appeared at these moments of history, and of all of them it can certainly be said that they have been dogmatists with authoritarian personalities. That suspicion also has been a factor has been evident in Leo I versus the Aryans, in Innocent versus the Albigensians, and in Pius IX and John Paul II versus the modern world. John Paul II is suspicious of intelligentsia (except for Cardinal Ratzinger) and of "foreigners," that is, non-Slavs; he actually speaks of the "American problem." Innocent III instituted the Inquisition; Pius IX's Vatican I atmosphere led to Pius X's "Vatican watchdogs," and John Paul II is still involved in the Inquisition, albeit on a more civilized level. Terror is part of suspicion. Those, like Gregory the Great and John XXIII, who struggled against authoritarian centralism, appeared to have open personalities that disliked dogma and its corresponding brutality. But, at particular moments, the anti-human demands of the practico-inert Church structure have required the authoritarian dogmatists in order that its structure be further centralized. Leo, Gregory VII, Innocent III, Pius IX and John Paul II, have been dogmatists and, therefore, have been the incarnation of the institution itself. They, in their biological and psychological selves, have been what the institution in its practico-inert self has been: oppressive, authoritarian, rigidly dogmatic, and apprehensive of any resemblance of freedom. The institution cannot do without individuals with their characteristics, nor can the individuals do without the institution. Thus, they are the institution and the institution is them.

The Present Church

Just as these Hildebrandian popes have served the institution of the Church extremely well, and have also been the incarnation of the Church in its most acute deviations, and insofar as the Church has been the receptacle of the preservation of the message of Jesus in Scriptures, so these men have been preservers of the message. But one must say that today the Church has become totally frozen, withdrawn and solitary.

The situation that necessitated the deviation of the Church's structure has changed. In fact, this situation changed long ago. Once the Enlightenment and the French Revolution introduced a new freedom into the West, and once public education made literacy a possibility for almost everyone, structures of authoritarian oppression really have been anachronistic. The Church, at the moment, is the most anachronistic.

For millions of Catholic Christians, the Church has become a negative element in the world, an element that is no longer capable of meaningful praxis. All change is responded to punitively and any form of change that was brought about by Vatican II is ultimately blocked and stagnated. To say that the Church has become a source of ignorance and lack of consciousness seems a bit extreme and unfair, but within the papacy of John Paul II, the incarnation of the present Church, the brilliance of the theologians and the courageous consciousness of religious women are punished and millions of married couples, in order to lead meaningful lives in the modern world, must ignore the dogmatic statements of a pope who truly appears to be ignorant of the situation of the modern world where over-population is strangling our planet, where pollution and deforestation are killing our planet, and where women everywhere are screaming to be free.

Conclusion

Now many questions can be asked. Can the dialectic of the praxis and of the intentions, of the visions and of the dreams that made early Christianity such a dynamic revolutionary force in the world be unfrozen? Can the anti-dialectical power of the deviations (or, rather, the one gigantic deviation that occurred) be transcended? All the deviations were part of one basic deviation: the substitution of the structure of love, of a free, open community of persons who were all part of the royal priesthood, for an extremely centralized, rigid, priestly caste-ridden hierarchical structure of domination, of sadism.

Can we have hope for the Church? Was there, within the institution, any praxis that never really deviated and that could, consequently, transform it? Is there any aspect of the original vision of Jesus Christ that has not deviated and that can, consequently, be the means of transcending the gigantic movement of circularity that the Church has been involved in for centuries? Can Catholic Christians within the Church gain control once more over a dialectical process that has been frozen by the process element of anti-praxis? Can a guided circularity be born? The Sartrean analysis of the Church of the preceding pages would appear to answer a strong "NO" to these questions. Certainly some individuals and some groups of Christians have kept the original vision alive: those involved in the liberation theology movement and various groups of American religious women and many theologians, but these persons and groups are rejected by the institution of the Church. They live the message of Jesus in spite of the Church. These individuals, who are the people of God, simply work around the Church, but can this situation supersede the original answer of "NO?" Is it true that the pure matter of *Being and Nothingness*, the being-in-itself, which can never be worked on by human praxis, that which lies beyond our knowledge, death itself, has thoroughly permeated the institution with impotence? The only question that then remains is, "What is to be done?"

9

What is to be Done?

Statement of the Problem

How can the dialectic of reason and of praxis, working as one praxis, unfreeze the structure of the Church so that the trap of circularity will be broken, so that the Gospel message of love will be enhanced, rather than distorted by that structure? In his *Critique of Dialectical Reason*, Sartre held before us the hope that dialectical reason has the ability ultimately to transcend its products, and since the structure of the Church is one of those products, it is then mandatory that this reason must struggle to attempt a solution that transcends the present Roman structure. Only dialectical reason can transcend such an anti-dialectical structure.

Since the structure of the institution, especially the structure of such an extremely hierarchalized institution, has greatly distorted the message of love that the Church preaches, another structure must be found that will allow that message to be communicated fully. The form of the group in fusion would seem to be the answer since, as we have seen in Chapter 3, that structure is the structure of love. But all the groups in fusion in history have always been of short duration. For this reason, if one is to think seriously in a dialectical manner about a structure that will allow the message of love to be freed from a structure created by deviation and circularity, and to flow through itself unimpeded, while still having some power of permanency, then, perhaps the best solution is to turn to Leonardo Boff's analysis of the Trinity in his book *Trinity and Society*.[1] Boff's Liberation Theology is a crucial factor in my proposal for radical church reform.

But first, it is necessary to review briefly the characteristics of the group in fusion, so that, even though the new structure cannot be a group in fusion, at least it will have no characteristics that fundamentally violate this structure of love. The structure must insure that: (*i*) no one can transcend anyone else, (*ii*) all will see the other as a subject, as oneself, (*iii*) all will have more or less the same project, (*iv*) all relations will be suffused with translucence and freedom and will be those of reciprocity, and (*v*) sovereignty will flow freely among all members.

Boff's Trinity

For Boff, God is a triune God composed of the Father, the Son and the Holy Spirit, who co-exist and are co-eternal. These Persons exist in perfect communion with one another, meaning that they are perfectly open to one another and "are one for one another" (*TS*, 5). This communion is so intense that it is "perichotic," that is, "each Person contains the other two, each one penetrates the others and is penetrated by them, one lives in the other" (*TS*, 5). The most active meaning of communion, and of perichoresis, Boff inherits from the Franciscan school of Bonaventure, Duns Scotus and William of Ockham and involves an "interweaving of one Person with the others and in the others" (*TS*, 136); it is "a permanent process of active reciprocity" (*TS*, 136). This communion, however, is just that. In other words, these Persons are truly different from one another, and a certain distance exists among them. In Sartrean terms, there are perfect relations of reciprocity and mutual recognition of the other one as oneself. Sovereignty flows freely among them; no short-circuiting occurs.

Although he is compelled by the nature of language to use diachronic words and phrases, such as the Father, knowing himself absolutely, communicates his own being to the Son, and the "Holy Spirit proceeds from an operation of the will of the Father and the Son" (*TS*, 91), Boff believes that one must, nevertheless, think synchronically. Instead of thinking in terms

---

1   Boff, Leonardo, *Trinity and Society*, trans. Paul Bruns (Maryknoll, NY: Orbis Books, 1988), 5. Hereinafter cited as "*TS*."

of the order of production, one must think in terms of "mutual revelation" (*TS*, 185). The co-existence and co-eternity of the Father, Son and Holy Spirit means that no temporal succession exists in God, for "God is [the] explosion and [the] implosion of life, intelligence and love" (*TS*, 90).

To demonstrate more clearly the significance of the Trinity, as depicted by Boff, one must look briefly at his analysis of the various heresies concerning the Trinity, as well as orthodox views that have a different stress, such as that of unity, as opposed to communion. Mention of these heresies is important for an understanding of what Boff rejects in his historical development of the concept of the Trinity. (*i*) *Modalism* was a heresy that stated that God reveals the self through three modes of revelation. What is lacking here is any form of communion. (*ii*) In the heresy of *subordinationism*, the Father is the only God. The Son and the Holy Spirit are simply subordinate creatures. This heresy, perhaps the most famous of all, was championed by Arius and is thus known as *Arianism*. Influenced by the Platonic philosophy that pervaded Alexandria, Arius taught that God is an absolutely transcendent and therefore incommunicable mystery that uses Christ as a mediator, but who, while being part of the divine sphere, is not God.

Even various orthodox notions about the Trinity are vulnerable to heresy. For example, in the early years of theological discussions, the concept of unity was stressed, for obvious historical reasons. What was emphasized was the Father's communicating his substance to the other Persons. Substance is that "which forms a permanent basis for all the differentiations that arise in it, or from it" (*TS*, 85). The danger here is subordinationism, an attitude that will caste the Father as the supreme monarch.

A similar problem arises in the idea of the original unity of a divine nature which each of the Persons appropriates to itself in distinct ways, or multiplies itself into "three hypostatic embodiments" (*TS*, 146). Such trinitarian monotheism has a monarchical structure, the roots of which are found in St. Ignatius of Antioch, who believed that "the celestial monarchy is the foundation for earthly monarchy" (*TS*, 153).

For Boff, the concept of "person," deeply rooted in our Latin past, is "one of the most significant achievements of Western culture" (*TS*, 86). The classical origins stressed "an existing subject (subsistent) distinct from others" (*TS*, 87). Medieval thinkers such as Duns Scotus stressed the incommunicability of the person. The modern emphasis is upon the concept of "being-for," a concept that sounds Sartrean. Modern thinkers make the most important aspect of "person" its structure of "orient[ation] toward others" (*TS*, 89). Boff claims that the identity of the "person" is "formed and completed on the basis of relationships with others" (*TS*, 89). "Interiority (consciousness in its ontological aspect) and openness to the other (freedom and the ethical dimension) constitute the mode of being proper to a person" (*TS*, 89). The interiority involves a centre of inner freedom that is always in tension with an orientation towards others. The result of this tension is that simultaneous with the eternal retaining of their differences, "the Father is fully in the Son and the Holy Spirit; the Son is fully in the Father and the Holy Spirit; the Holy Spirit is fully in the Father and the Son" (*TS*, 93). This tension, thus, is the reality of perichoresis, an eternally dynamic process. Since "God is ... the living One" (*TS*, 124), perichoresis is the reality of life, for as Boff states, "Christian faith professes that the primary Reality is not undifferentiated eternal life, but eternal life gushing out as Father, Son and Holy Spirit" (*TS*, 127).

Thus, in summary, for Boff, "communion," that which is "proper to beings gifted with a spiritual nature" (*TS*, 129), is the concept through which one begins to understand the meaning of person and the meaning of God. The ultimate basis of reality is the communion of the three Persons of the Trinity, "not to be found in the solitude of One" (*TS*,139), and that communion is love.

In order to make clear the differences within this group, Boff describes briefly what qualities are unique for each Person. "Utterly mysterious depth" distinguishes the Father; "the [revelation of the] Father, manifest as Wisdom" distinguishes the Son, and "the power of love" distinguishes the Holy Spirit (*TS*, 146, 147). Thus, relations with the Father involve a movement toward the past of one's origins; relations with the Son involve a transcending movement, a movement outward toward others; relations with the Holy Spirit involve a movement inward toward "the depths of one's own personality" (*TS*, 149). We, as creatures of the Earth, are "an aspect of his [the Son's] complete revelation" (*TS*, 186), an aspect of this outward movement.

Sartre's Dialectic

Now, the task is to apply Sartre's dialectical reason to the theoretical construct of Boff to see if it is possible to conceive of a structure for the new Church that would reflect love, but one, unlike that of the group in fusion, that would not be a fleeting existence. Boff's construct is, according to Christian theology, at its very root, the construct of love; therefore, what must be done is to use Sartre's dialectic to think through to a concrete manifestation of this construct. If this particular construct of love can be thought through the structure of dialectical reason, perhaps this reason can transcend its product, the present Church structure, and then, consequently, build a new concrete structure of love, rather than of sado-masochism.

But first, it is necessary to take a brief look at what Sartre's dialectic entails. An overview of the concept was given in the previous chapter, but now, a more in-depth analysis is needed. For Sartre, the praxis of the individual is a microcosm of an overall view of history. This praxis, which is dialectical, takes place in concrete situations. Individuals find themselves in a particular set of material conditions and wish to change them. In the process of this change, the conscious actions of individuals move from the original set of external circumstances to the set of new conditions that have just been brought into being. The praxis moves from one external moment to another. But, as Sartre tells us in his *Search for a Method*,[2] in order for the movement to culminate in the second external moment, the conscious movement must pass through the subjectivity of the individual (*SM*, 97) Thus, the basic elements of praxis are both objective and subjective. Praxis always involves human consciousness interacting with the external world through concrete action. Thus, consciousness and action are one within praxis (*CDR*, I:93). One sees here the embryo of Sartre's idea that the movement of history and the kind of consciousness necessary to understand history are both dialectical. In other words, it is the oneness of consciousness and the external world in praxis on a micro scale that we can see Sartre's union of these same elements in the concrete movement of history and its subsequent intelligibility on a macro scale.

The structure of praxis forms the basic structure of the project. Upon this basis, Sartre builds a more complex structure, both synchronically and diachronically. In other words, the structure is more complex than that of praxis in relation to space and time. Whereas praxis involves the movement of an action from one set of external conditions to another through the subjectivity of the individual, the project involves not only the same kind of structured movement, but also the actual surpassing by individuals of their present objective conditions toward new objective conditions. A more concrete spatial element is added. But even more important, the structure of the concept of change appears. Not surprisingly, change is dialectical; it involves elements of human consciousness and external material reality.

---

2 Sartre, Jean-Paul, *Search for a Method*, trans. Hazel E. Barnes (New York: Vintage Press, 1968). Hereinafter cited as "*SM*"; originally published in French as "Question de Méthode," the prefatory essay to the French edition of *Critique of Dialectical Reason, Volume I*.

The synchronic (spatial) structure of the project expands when Sartre further explains that the project also involves a movement (through the subjectivity of the individual) between the objective conditions of the environment that the individual will surpass and the objective struc- tures that Sartre calls "the field of possibles" (*SM*, 135). The dialectical objective-subjective-objective movement that we first saw within praxis has intensified, has become more multifaceted. The "field of possibles" is quite different from "material conditions," although the former may often overlap with the latter. The field of possibles is composed of any aspect of the world of consciousness and of the world of material condi- tions that individuals may use in order to initiate the movement of praxis for the purpose of superseding present material conditions.

Simultaneous with the enrichment and increasing complexity of the synchronic movement of the dialectic within the project is the enrichment and increasing complexity of the diachronic movement as it expands greatly through time. When one confronts the field of possibles within the project, one confronts not only the field of the present historical moment in which one lives, but also, the future fields of possibles. These fields move toward the present field, in- forming it with the structures of the future. For Sartre, the presence of these future structures has an extremely powerful influence upon the individual (*SM*, 96). Sartre goes so far as to imply that these future fields of possibles are perhaps the most powerful influence. The future moves toward the present field, while the individual moves toward the future. To involve oneself with the project is to involve oneself automatically with the future. But the dialectical movement also extends itself toward the past, which it transcends and preserves (*SM*, 105, 106).

Since the movements of praxis, of the project, and of history itself, which is created by the collective praxis of individuals, are dialectical, in order to understand history, one must develop dialectical reason. To think dialecti- cally, one must be able: (*i*) to think the movement within praxis and within the project; (*ii*) to think the dialectical movement in its passage from the objectivity of the external world, through the subjectivity of the individual, and back to the external world – the most fundamental aspect of the process; and (*iii*) to think the movement as it expands synchronically to embrace the field of possibles and as it expands diachronically to embrace the past and the future.

The most fundamental aspect of the dialectic of history is the dialec- tic that exists between the individual and the external world. Within the structure of every praxis and of every project, individuals must become the means for transforming the environment.

The Sartrean Dialectic of Boff's Trinity

Now, having summarized briefly the Sartrean dialectic, the first question to ask is whether or not Boff's construct is dialectical in the Sartrean sense. That is, if one can think the construct through in terms of dialectical reason, one can say that there is hope for the creative transcending of the present Church structure. Upon observing the triune construct of God, the first objection would be that God is eternal, and, consequently, can have nothing to do with the dialectic of history. But this triune God becomes historical with the incarnation of the Son as Jesus; therefore, it is now possible to entertain the idea of the dialectic of history in relation to the Trinity. Having surpassed that objection, one must first look at the synchronic aspect of the dialectic. Following Boff's construct, one can say that each Person of the Trinity, in relating to the two others, is constantly involved in an intense dialectic. Viewing the dialectic from the subjectivity of the Son, one sees the Son as constantly relating to the objectivities of the Father and of the Holy Spirit. For example, in the grand project of love, the objectivity of the Father will pass through the subjectivity of the Son in its movement from itself to the objectivity of the Holy Spirit. The objectivity of the Holy Spirit will pass through the subjectivity of the Son in its movement from itself to the objectivity of the Father, etc.

Thus, the basic movement of the internal relations of the Trinity is the very movement of the foundation of the synchronic aspect of dialectical reason. This movement expands as it enters history where the second objective moment is added, the embracing of the field of possibles, which includes all creation. This embrace, the project of loving all creation, is so powerful that the movement of love surpasses old conditions toward the new. Creation is constantly renewed. Life constantly springs forth. Constant change is everywhere.

Second, one must look at the diachronic aspect of the dialectic. The diachronic movement must be toward a past that is constantly preserved and transcended, as well as toward a future whose promise shapes it while simultaneously sending it back toward itself so that it can gradually concretize this promise. Again, once one views the Trinity operating within history through the Incarnation, the problem of the diachronic movement begins to disappear, but, nevertheless, one must investigate to see if such a movement occurs. If the Father is the Person whose primary movement is toward a past of origins, one begins to see part of this dialectic, for this movement would have to involve the constant return to the present from this past, as well as a preserving and transcending of this past. A preserving action must occur, for the concept of annihilating any part of the past relationship of the Trinity is unthinkable within the framework of Christian theology. A transcending action will also occur, for the very essence of the Trinity is life, the act of living, and anything that is constantly living must constantly transcend the past and what the past in its fullest form means, i.e., death. Since all Persons share a radical orientation toward the future, for their relationship in its fulfilled form is the promise of the realized kingdom of the future, this triune relationship constantly moves dialectically toward and back from that future. Thus, the triune God follows the basic structures of Sartre's dialectical reason. Now, one can think the construct of Boff's triune God of love through dialectical reason.

The Anti-Dialectical Structure of the Church

Once it has been established that Boff's triune God follows the movement of Sartre's dialectical reason, the problem is to use this dialectic to transcend the structure of the Church as it now exists. But before attempting this difficult task, one must pause briefly to note that no part of the structure of the present Church is dialectical. All movement begins at the top of the pyramid; any attempt for those at the bottom to create a movement back to the top is stifled.

For example, synchronically speaking, the pope and his immediate advisors, from the point of view of their subjectivity, allow their reason to move from this subjectivity to an objectivity. Sometimes that objectivity is the entire Church; sometimes it is particular individuals or particular parts of the Church. What is wrong is that the movement is not from objectivity through subjectivity toward another objectivity. Instead, there is a movement from subjectivity to objectivity.

Diachronically speaking, especially under the influence of Cardinal Ratzinger, the reason of the pope and his advisors constantly moves back to the Cardinal's understanding of thirteenth-century Thomistic philosophy and then back to the present. This thirteenth-century philosophy is certainly preserved, but it is not transcended. This non-transcendence makes the movement of reason to the future impossible. Thus, all those openings to the future presented to them from the sciences and the social sciences are flatly rejected. The consequence is that the present structure does not pass the Sartrean dialectical test.

If the structure of the new Church is to be formed according to dialectical reason, it will move freely with the dialectic of history itself. One can argue that, for a certain period of time, the structure of the Church closely paralleled the history in which it existed. But, until the early Middle Ages, the structure of the Church was not nearly as frozen as it is now. This structure reached its peak in the thirteenth century. But at the Council of Trent it becomes obvious that the structure of the Church was not coincident with the movement of history. It was at this moment that history began to move into its truly modern period, a period that is marked by its fast-moving diachronic dynamism. But it is just such a diachronic dynamism that the Church's structure lacked; consequently, it is at this moment that one notices that a strange gap existed between the Church and history. Since the structure was non-dialectical, it could not move with history, because, according to Sartre, in spite of the occasional presence of anti-dialectical movements, history is dialectical. Whether or not a new Church will be open to history will depend upon whether or not this Church will have a structure that is dialectical. Thus, what lies before us is what seems the unthinkable task of allowing dialectical reason to construct this new structure. Then, the question can be asked, "Does this structure have at least some of the basic characteristics of the group in fusion?"

One cautionary note must be sounded before bringing forth a concrete proposal. Since the group in fusion as a proposal for an overall Church structure is not practical at this moment in history, any reasonably permanent structure will have to take on the qualities of some form of institution. One can argue that the grass roots or base communities that originated in Brazil contradict Sartre's comments about the fleetingness of such groups, for they appear to be groups in fusion that have exhibited signs of permanence, but it does not seem possible that this grass roots structure can be duplicated on the scale that will be needed in order to include the entire world Church.

Nevertheless, in what follows, I would like to propose a structure that aims to eliminate the rigid hierarchy of the present Church – probably one of the most "institutionalized institutions" on earth. To create some elements of democracy and modern thinking within the structure of the Church is the modest hope of this exercise. The goal is to construct a structure that will not be institutionalized in any way, but such an undertaking must be the work of the Holy Spirit, through the collective work of the Church membership in some future time. The following proposal is simply one small step in that direction.

An Immodest Concrete Proposal

Obviously, the first place to begin is to dispose of a structure that allows reason to flow only in one direction synchronically and that, in a sense, only has a uni-directional movement in time. What must be established in its place is the same kind of structure as Boff sees in the Trinity. But, first, this structure must pass the test of whether it can replace the uni-directionalism of reason that exists within the present structure and its singular diachronic dialectic with the past with an intense dialectic of reason that includes a diachronic dialectic with the future.

In more concrete terms, at the focal point of Boff's model is de-centralization. The monarch God has disappeared into a triune form. De-centralization is necessary if the synchronic dialectic is going to flow in an objective-subjective-objective manner. Such a movement is neces-sary if authoritarianism is to be prevented. In general terms, to elimi-nate the first objective aspect is to eliminate the present reality of the world from one's subjectivity, and thus to eliminate any possibility of dialogue with that world. Since history takes place in the world, to elimi-nate the first objective moment of the dialectic is to eliminate any possi-bility of dialogue with that world.

Since the entire Church must be included within this decentralized structure, the laity is also included. At the present moment, the laity and, in fact, all women are excluded. Such decentralization means that the present structure of the hierarchy must be dismantled. A structure must be in place, but there is no room for the kind of hierarchy that exists now.

In an attempt to interweave Boff's model and Sartrean dialectics, I propose three fundamental sections of the Church: one composed of theologians, one of bishops (half of whom, ideally, would be women), and a third composed of laity. Each group would have elected repre-sentatives in one central location. There would be a governing council in which each group would have equal representation, a council that, in turn, would elect a person to be its head for a limited number of years. That person could be a theologian, a bishop, or a lay person, and, of course, gender would be irrelevant.

In order to make certain that the Sartrean synchronic dialectic is in place, I must emphasize the role of the laity. These are the persons who will observe the present world and who will make certain that all dis-cussion of matters within the council begin in that world and not in some subjective world that exists within the mind of male popes, cardi-nals and bishops who live in a thirteenth-century fantasy. Once such an objective pole is established, dialectical reason will move from that pole, the pole of history, to the minds of the representatives within the coun-cil who will then ponder that pole within the interiority of their beings. Then, after consideration and discussion, the hope will be that dialectical reason will move toward a truly objective field of possibles whose vari-ous alternatives will be able, for the first time since early church history, to present themselves clearly. It is at that moment that the council will be able to choose from that objective field of possibles a concrete solution that will act upon a world from which that solution has been born, rather than from a mind whose formation is based upon the high Middle Ages.

The following dialectic will have taken place: (*i*) The decisions of the council will have been born in the original objective moment in the present world. (*ii*) These decisions will have gone through a gestation that has involved a subjective moment that, in turn, will return to that objective world to examine the field of possibles. (*iii*) Then, the final decisions, another subjective moment, of that council, will return to and affect the objective present world. Although never perfect, since perfection is something that belongs to the fulfilled kingdom, these decisions will, at least, bear some resemblance to the situation to which they are addressing themselves. Consequently, the reason of the representatives of the council will be in a synchronic dialectical movement with the objective world, with history itself.

Among both the representatives of the laity and the theologians, in order to have a greater sense of the diachronic dialectic of reason that must be coincident with that of history, there must be historians, those who will be conversant with the past to such an extent that they will understand what must be preserved and what must be transcended. It is this understanding of the past, plus the openness to the present world through the two objective moments within the synchronic dialectic of reason, that will then allow the reason of the council and all those that they represent to move toward the future of promise, the future that beckons us toward the fulfillment of the kingdom. Then, in fulfillment of the Sartrean dialectic itself, the movement of the diachronic dialectic toward the future will return to the present moment. The result will be that the members of the council will then be in touch with the future kingdom, with a world that is more humane, more loving, more just, rather than with a distant past world that would probably make us shudder with horror if we were able to see beyond the beauty of its cathedrals and universities. This future sensibility will free the council members and, thus, the entire Church, from the bondage of the past, which so oppresses the present Church. This future sensibility will allow these persons to be able to see more clearly what aspects of the past must be transcended in order for the Church to fulfill its mission. But, most importantly, this sensibility will allow the trap of circularity to be broken, the circularity, with its absorption of past practico-inerts that is so essential to the Church's deviation from the Gospel message. Thus, the representatives of the council will be involved in a diachronic dialectical movement with history.

Next, the dialectical reason test must be applied to the internal relations of the group. In Sartrean terms, the subjectivity of the bishops' group will be penetrated by the objectivity of the lay group and the theological group, just as the subjectivity of the lay group will be penetrated by the objectivity of the two other groups. From the point of view of the bishop's group, for example, the synchronic movement of the dialectic will begin with the objective moment of the lay group, will pass through the subjective moment of the bishops' group, and then will pass to the objective moment of the theological group. One can also reverse the procedure, having the objective moment begin with the theological group and end with the objective moment of the lay group or begin with the objective moment of the bishops' group, which will then pass through the subjective moment of the lay group to the objective moment of the theological group, etc. Thus, an internal synchronic dialectic operates among the internal perichotic relations of these groups.

Now, it is necessary to examine the relationship between members of the council and those whom they represent. Choosing representatives from among theologians will simply mean that various theological organizations will come together at regular intervals to arrange for an election by all its members. The representatives for the bishops will be elected, not only by bishops, but also by all priests and nuns, whether diocesan, or in orders. Within this Church, all bishops will have been elected previously by the priests, nuns and laity within a particular diocese. The election of the lay members will be arranged through parishes. Parish councils can select persons, whose names will be sent to regional councils, who, in turn, will elect lay persons from among these recommendations to the council at the Vatican. Thus, a synchronic dialectic will be set up between each group at the council and the grass roots constituents in various parishes, convents, monasteries and universities throughout the world. At the present moment, within the structure of the Church, these constituents are only the objective moment that receives directives from the subjective moment that exists at the top of the pyramid. But, in the new Church, these constituents will be not only the first objective moment in the world that the council will have to take into consideration, but also, through the election of their representatives, they will take part indirectly in the subjective moment of the council. The synchronic element of the dialectic will act within a truly world-wide dimension.

But, in order to give this synchronic element a fully, meaningful multidimensionality that is truly representative of the objective world, a specified number of non-Church members, that is, non-Catholic: Protestant, Jewish, Hindu, Buddhist, Moslem, or atheist, should be included within the theological and lay groups. In other words, ecumenism will be built into the structure for these members will have voting rights. Advisory power is not power. In order for the ecumenism to have meaning, the non-Church members should have voting rights. The theological organizations, many of which already are ecumenical, will elect these non-Church members. Of course, the parish councils will select only Church members as possible representatives. It is only within such a far-reaching synchronic dialectic that one can say for the first time in hundreds of years that the Church will be truly in touch with the first moment of the movement of the synchronic dialectic in the objective world, and with history, for it is in this objective world that history is created. Finally, the modern Church will have a structure modeled on dialectical reason that will coincide with the dialectical movement of history.

Now that one can say that the concrete model of the new Church has the structure of Sartre's dialectical reason, it is necessary to examine whether or not this concrete model coincides with Boff's concept of the love which exists within the Triune God. The entire purpose of this project is to determine what structure for a new Church can be a structure of love that will replace the present sado-masochistic structure.

For Boff, once again, the structure of the triune God is "perichotic"; there is complete interpenetration of all three persons by the other persons. Within this new structure, such interpenetration among all three groups, quite distinct from one another, will be possible since, through the representatives of all three groups, full, open and complete dialogue will always be possible. Thus, a communion among all three groups will exist. Although no one can expect the exact reflection of the perfect communion of the Trinity, a safeguard for as much communion as possible will be put in place by the fact that no group can have power over the other. No structure of domination will exist. In theological terms, all three groups will co-exist and will be co-eternal. For example, the bishops' group will be committing, in Boff's terms, the heresy of *subordinationism* if they try to place themselves in a position of superiority. *Arianism* will not be permitted. To envision the theological or lay group as being entities that have appropriated, in distinct ways, the power and position of the bishops' group will be to succumb to the trinitarian monotheism, the roots of St. Ignatius of Antioch, the kind of thinking that helped to set up the structure that now exists.

Boff's claim that each person of the Trinity, to demonstrate its personhood, must be "orient[ed] toward others" (*TS*, 89) implies that the three groups of the new Church structure, having passed the Sartrean synchronic dialectical test, will each behave as a person. In other words, the basic movement from the objective (external world in general), through the subjective moment of reflection upon the (objective) field of possibles and a subsequent (subjective) decision toward the objective moment of creating change in the world is the structure of orientation toward others. The constant praxis of each group is orientation toward the other groups and toward the world, a praxis that will involve the embracing of fields of possibles in order to institute change. Here, Boff's concern of orientation toward others is satisfied within the objective moments of Sartre's dialectic. Boff's concern with "interiority" is satisfied within the subjective moment.

Thus, real communion will exist among all groups, which in Boff's terms implies openness, reciprocity, immediacy, and the accepting of differences. Lay status and gender will no longer prevent the overwhelming majority of Church members from participating in the full life of the Church. Such a life will be far more dynamic than that which exists at present because the reciprocity of three persons (groups) produces a dynamism that the "solitude of One" (TS, 139) cannot produce.

Now that the new structure has fulfilled Boff's criteria for communion/love, it is necessary to submit it to Sartre criteria. According to Sartre's Being and Nothingness, the first step in the creation of love is an attempt, in response to the look of the other, to incorporate the transcendence of the other person within oneself. One asks the beloved to accept oneself as "the whole World" (BN, 479), as the absolute value which he can never transcend. Then, one's independence is assured. The beloved founds one's essence and one recovers the freedom which was lost in the first moment of the "look." The lover, in turn, must maintain the subjectivity of the beloved in order for the beloved to identify the lover with his freedom. But the lover must remain an object to him, for the ideal is always to be other to oneself, a situation which is the purpose of a relationship with the other. One always longs to found one's own being, to give to oneself freely one's being-in-itself as other.

Within the new Church structure, no group would attempt to transcend the other groups. Instead, the transcendence of the other groups would be incorporated into each group, without removing from it its character as transcendence. Furthermore, in insisting upon remaining at all times an objective moment that both begins and ends the dialectical movement within the triune group, each group would remain an object for the other groups, and, in so doing, each group would become the unsurpassable, the source of all values that the other groups could never transcend. Thus, the independence of each group is assured, and, consequently, no group can claim that its group existed prior to that of any other, and thus claim domination over the others.

Each group must and would maintain the subjectivity, the source of the transcendence, of the others. In other words, each group would allow the other groups to enjoy a subjective moment within the dialectic and, subsequently, allow the other group to found its essence. The present structure of the Church allows no subjective moment to exist for either the laity or for theologians, other than those who are immediate advisors of the papacy. As well, this moment of subjectivity would allow each group to identify and to maintain the freedom of the other groups. Because each group can identify with the freedom of the other groups, it can remain other to itself, and, in some manner, as much as is possible outside of the fulfilled kingdom, become "the very being of the ontological proof – that is, God" (*BN*, 476).

Thus, through analyzing the new structure of the Church within the framework of Sartrean theory, this structure complies with the structure of his concept of love and with his structure of dialectical reason. Also, through analyzing the new structure of the Church within the framework of Boff's concept of the Trinity (his concept of love and communion), one finds that the structure of the new Church complies with Boff's concepts founded upon the model of the triune God.[3]

Finally, one must ask how closely this new structure compares with the group in fusion. Within the new structure, no possibility exists for one group of persons to transcend another. Sovereignty flows freely among all aspects of the triune structure. Since all relations among these aspects are reciprocal, all relations will be those of translucence and freedom. All persons will see the others as themselves. The overall project will be the same, but because of the size of the structure and the complexity of the project, a certain division of labour will be necessary. Absolute paralleling of projects will be impossible. Furthermore, because some form of stability must be built into the structure, there should be a leader elected for a limited term. This situation means that, even though this person will not be allowed to transcend the other persons, because of the movement of dialectical reason, her transcendence/immanence position (the position of all persons in a group in fusion) will tend slightly more toward transcendence than will that of the momentary leader in a group in fusion, and, consequently, assurances must be built into the

---

3 Sartre's claim that God's existence is an impossibility, or, in Sartre's terms from *Being and Nothingness*, that the being-in-itself-for-itself's existence is an impossibility, is interesting, but not relevant here, for Sartre's inquiry into the structures of existence does not commit one to either a definitive atheisic or theistic position. The structures that he gives us are sufficiently broad to lay the foundation for such an analysis as Boff's. What is relevant here is that the structure of the new church can be analyzed through the historical categories of existence that Sartre explores, through Sartrean tools. To use these tools to analyze a love that has a theistic basis is simply to apply Sartre's analytical tools to an historical structure.

structure to maintain strongly the immanence pull upon the leader. Also, the necessity of building in some form of permanence into the new structure means that inertia will be present that is not manifested in the group in fusion. But since the movement of dialectical reason, according to Sartre, is the law of creative transcendence of matter and of the practico-inert, a constant transcendence of this inertia can be maintained.

This new structure may only be one step toward a better structure that persons of the future will forge from a future field of possibles that has more alternatives than the present field. Nevertheless, this new structure should, at least for the present, be a conduit through which the Gospel message of love can pass, rather than a sado-masochistic structure which obstructs that message from being fulfilled in any meaningful manner within the world. The form must match the content. Although the structure may not be made always of crystal or of diamond, but may, at times, be made only of glass through which one can see darkly, at least the Church will be a true lover who will call me, a lover who will not threaten, but rather, will safeguard my transcendence, will found my being, will identify with my freedom, will, at least, partially satisfy my desire to be like the gods. Then, my demon lover, whose present call, if answered, would try to crush my transcendence, threaten my being and place my freedom in chains, would be converted to the true lover that the future fulfilled kingdom, the city of diamonds, has always promised.

Index

145